BULLISH ON BITCOIN

37 STRATEGIES TO PROFIT IN THE NEW CRYPTO ECONOMY

Misha Yurchenko

Copyright © 2018 by Misha Yurchenko.

All rights reserved. No part of this publication may be reproduced, distributed or transmitted in any form or by any means, including photocopying, recording, or other electronic or mechanical methods, without the prior written permission of the publisher, except in the case of brief quotations embodied in critical reviews and certain other noncommercial uses permitted by copyright law.

ISBN 9781790211586 (paperback)

www.mishayurchenko.me/crypto-resources/

BONUS MATERIAL

As a free gift I've compiled a list of resources for your crypto journey:

1. The best 39 books to delve into all aspects of blockchain and the world of cryptocurrencies.
2. 100 + resources for traders and investors, including a list of trading and investment tools.
3. A smart trading journal that you can use to keep track of your trades.
4. A technical analysis guide book + cheat sheet to identify price action, and entry and exit points.
5. A list of my favorite blockchain podcasts, videos and blog posts.
6. A list of raw, unedited transcripts with 30 blockchain CEOs.
7. All of the links and URLs included in the citations for easy access.

Visit this link to get the list:
www.mishayurchenko.me/crypto-resources/

TABLE OF CONTENTS

Introduction 1

PART 1: TRADING 15

Chapter 1. Know Thyself 17
Chapter 2. The Only Trading Strategy You Will Ever Need 31
Chapter 3. Dr. Jekyll and Mr. Hyde 49
Chapter 4. 10 Lessons From an Expert Crypto Investor 63
Chapter 5. Five Things Bruce Lee Taught Me About Trading 73
Chapter 6. Create Systems, Not Goals 81
Chapter 7. Your Risk Management Plan 87

PART II: 37 STRATEGIES TO PROFIT IN THE NEW CRYPTO ECONOMY 101

PART III: INVESTING 161

Chapter 1. The Investor's Guide to Evaluating Cryptoassets 163
Chapter 2. My Process in Action: Why I Invested $11,250 in 0x ... 181
Chapter 3. 17 Times People Were Totally Wrong About the Future ... 193
Chapter 4. Never Give Up Your Railroads 201
Chapter 5. 11 Investment Tips to Remember 207
Chapter 6. Tokenizing the World 221
Chapter 7. The Tried and True Path to Riches: Build a Career 233
Chapter 8. What I Learned From 30 Blockchain CEOs 241

Parting Words...Think Long Term 251
Authors Love Reviews 253
Resources and Recommendations 255
Glossary of Terms 261
Acknowledgements 265

INTRODUCTION

BROKEN PROMISES

It was a week before Christmas and all through crypto land investors were giddy as bitcoin soared past $19,000 USD. The media was merrily writing articles about the new digital coin traded among peers. Families huddled around the Internet reading the latest tweets and Facebook updates and talked about the possibilities. They fumbled through explanations of blockchain, debated the identity of Satoshi Nakamoto and talked of the prospects of a new economic meritocracy taking over from the banks and other leeches whose fees sucked money from the poor. Kids opened Coinbase accounts for their parents. Grandma was day trading. CNBC added a special bitcoin feature. Hundreds of millions of people were tuning in.

The 2008 financial crisis was a low point, but something great emerged from the ashes in 2009—inflation-proof digital money. We didn't make a full comeback, but nobody was thinking about the past. Their eyes were set on the future of bitcoin. This was a chance to unlock a door which had been inaccessible since the Medici's—a 15th century banking family—financed commerce, large cathedrals and great works of art across Europe; money was controlled by greedy, centralized banks that nobody liked. The mere possibility that the system could be disintermediated was automatically intriguing. Free from the shackles of tyrannical rule and authority over what was rightfully ours all along.

But really, we were most excited about the stories of bitcoin millionaires, and we wanted a piece of that sweet, sweet pie. Bitcoin had already become the fastest growing financial asset in history. CME Bitcoin Futures announced their launch, and other cryptocurrency futures markets followed. Venture capitalists dropped their jaws as ICOs raised billions of dollars with zero working product (just the 'idea'). Facebook feeds were inundated with Serbian cryptocurrency video ads. *The Wall Street Journal* created a prototype for their cryptocurrency—WSJ Coin. Social media platforms like Reddit were raving about bitcoin.

The day of the CME launch, December 10th 2017, bitcoin soared to almost $20,000. It was up five times from its price just three weeks earlier. Other coins made substantially higher gains in the 10-20x multiple range. Trading volume continued to increase. This marked the peak. And then the market did what all markets do—it corrected. And to the disbelief of many, it kept going down. Investors panicked. Sentiment took a 180-degree turn overnight. Everything after that can be only described as a bloodbath. Millions were made and lost in a period of days.

What really happened? How were the futures markets involved? Did so-called whales manipulate price action? Or was it just an inevitable fall after savvy traders realized we were at an unsustainable high? Nobody knows for certain. One thing is for sure, though. The currencies, while digital, had repercussions in the real world. Real mortgages and real loans were taken out to fill crypto coffers. People lost money. They rage-quit on Twitter and moved into their parents' basements. Talking heads came out of the woodwork. This was just like the

17th century Dutch "Tulip Mania," they said. History was repeating itself. No, it was worse. Bitcoin was "rat poison squared," said Warren Buffett. The tax-man scratched his head but showed no mercy taxing cryptocurrency gains. Acid was poured into the wounds.

The get-rich-quick scheme had not panned out; well, at least not for most. Those who cashed out in time went on to buy lambos (or just stole money raised in ICOs and disappeared), but many others put their money to work and started tech companies of their own. The less fortunate took verbal beatings from their friends ("I told you so!"), deleted their Coinmarketcap apps and went back to their day jobs. Was bitcoin a broken promise? After all, there was no practical use for a currency so volatile. Cashing out your crypto was not easy. Your money was still taxable and controlled by centralized banks. Mining used up too much electricity and was bad for the environment. A majority of bitcoin was in the hands of a few, so how could we say that it was truly decentralized?

Now that the dust has settled, it's easier to see what happened. We can take a breath of fresh air and look around us to answer these questions.

PLUCKING THE WEEDS

The 2000 dot-com edition of the Monopoly board game is full of companies that I barely remember, like iVillage and Lycos. You'll also recognize some of them—Expedia and Monster—and I'd say the Monopoly guys did a decent job at picking companies that are still around. Except for one problem. Google, Amazon, Facebook and Apple weren't even on the board. It was simply too early. Many of the companies on the board lost dominance and others like Excite were later acquired.

Like the dot-com bust, during the crypto bubble, many projects died a necessary death. Most ICOs were fluff. After regulators came in, it was the end for many exchanges. Only a handful of projects remained. The top 50 crypto projects by market cap are markedly different today than they were at the start of 2018; and they were markedly different one year before that, and the year before that. The word 'blockchain' is no longer popular in company earnings calls. CEOs scaled down blockchain engineering efforts when they realized they could do well with a plain old database. So does this portend the end of the blockchain? Not at all.

Remember the Medicis? Their empire fell but the double ledger accounting system they invented is still used today. Likewise, Bitcoin may one day be minuscule in value to those that run different blockchain platforms, but the blockchain digital ledger will prevail. Almost all major companies are exploring blockchain implementations.

Many of the big blockchain projects that will dominate the future haven't even been born yet. From this perspective the dot-com bust is a fair comparison. It reminds me of Pets.com—the darling of the Internet boom. It failed but online pet stores have grown into one of the largest e-commerce sectors.

Before you see sustained growth, you need what one startup founder describes as the "1000 Flowers Blooming" stage of an industry (sometimes I feel the world of crypto is very floral). It implies that many ideas, projects and businesses are required to jumpstart the whole ecosystem. After a while, most of the flowers are revealed to be weeds. But a few of them turn out to be roses, and those are the ones we hope to pick.

The pain of financial loss was amplified because ICOs and bitcoin were accessible to practically everyone; Peruvian farmer and Wall

INTRODUCTION

Street trader alike. That was at least one difference between the dot-com bust, and one reason it was more devastating to the average Joe. Bitcoin is like the social media of money, and while it has its positives, the virality factor has spread news rapidly and created much fear, uncertainty and doubt. This is a necessary part of the process and evolution of a new industry.

> *"Just because a market is in a "bubble" doesn't mean it's going to die. Bitcoin has been through over half a dozen big bubbles and increased in price after each one."*
> —CHRIS DUNN

BEYOND GREAT STORYTELLING

Every time there's a new issue that pops up (scalability, regulation, transaction costs, security, etc.), solutions are proposed. Bitcoin becoming money is still a great story, and as the incessant social media chatter reveals, everyone has an opinion. But the narrative delves deeper into the real purpose and value of Bitcoin. Consider these Bitcoin narratives around the world.

Look at the millions of people in Venezuela who trust Bitcoin over their local currency, and even the US dollar. Bitcoin is not the best store of value—if Venezuelans could, they'd buy US dollars, which are more stable sources of value. However, it's dangerous to hold USD. The government could come in and seize their money. Bitcoin solves this problem, although not perfectly, but for an unstable government the store of value is "good enough." Similarly, the love of the Chinese for decentralized cryptocurrencies is a solution to Chinese governmental control. There are substantial restrictions in China for people moving money between banks and into other currencies.

Many Chinese people are happy to move their money into crypto rather than keep it in local currency.

We often don't think about restrictions on the free flow of money in the West because we have relatively stable banks. We have to take a step back and realize that there are over 1 billion people who don't have bank accounts in the world. There are many others who live in countries (that have much bigger populations than the US) where they simply don't trust their governments, and the same rules don't apply. This is a much bigger factor than you might realize if you're living in a developed country.

> *"...poverty is not the result of rapacious financiers exploiting the poor. It has much more to do with the lack of financial institutions, with the absence of banks, not their presence. Only when borrowers have access to efficient credit networks can they escape from the clutches of loan sharks, and only when savers can deposit their money in reliable banks can it be channelled from the idle rich to the industrious poor."*
> —NIALL FERGUSON, THE ASCENT OF MONEY: A FINANCIAL HISTORY OF THE WORLD

In this meritocracy, uncontrolled by authority, no one owns the narrative and it can change. The narratives are more fluid and blockchain solutions evolve faster to meet market demand. Change is evolutionary.

Nonetheless, a lot of people are waiting for a sort of "flippening," or for other projects to take over Bitcoin's market cap. This is certainly possible, but first-mover advantage plays a big role. Why did gold become gold? Titanium and platinum are more rare and could have been competitors, but at some point in history gold was recognized as the default currency of trade and has lasted for 5,000 years. It's not that gold is the best, just like bitcoin, but it had a first mover advantage.

When you think about bitcoin as a brand, it may not be the best, but the best product does not always win. The average investor will probably start with bitcoin, and a company that is starting to accept crypto for payments will probably use bitcoin.

BITCOIN IS DEAD

Maybe you're skeptical, burnt, tired. You've lost money or have friends who have lost money. I often speak to people who regret not getting into crypto early. They lose sleep over it. They wish they would have bought bitcoin at $1 when their nerdy friend had mentioned it years ago. Life would have been a lot different. Big houses, Asian wives and purple lambos. *Shoulda, coulda, woulda.* These are the same people who saw bitcoin at $100 and declared matter-of-factly that "the ship had sailed!"

Then, when bitcoin hit $1,000, they thought, "Oh, no way the price is sustainable." They didn't buy then, either. When bitcoin quintupled and hit $5,000, skeptical minds stubbornly prevailed. Egos were torn. At the same time, they got more salty, bitter, angry and resentful. They could have bought at $100, but their pessimism and pride had put up the worst kind of mental roadblock. Making excuses is easy.

Every year people scream "bitcoin is dead!" and every year they're wrong; in fact, they've been wrong 323 times according to the list of 'Bitcoin Obituaries.'[1] I take the news with a very microscopic grain of salt. The common objections to cryptocurrencies have been addressed

---

1 "Bitcoin Obituaries," 99bitcoin.com, https://99bitcoins.com/bitcoin-obituaries/

many times over. From it being "bad for the environment"[2] (energy consumption is moving towards a much more efficient decentralized model; and there are far greater environmental costs involved when you use your credit card, bank or AWS data center-fueled services), to bitcoin is being "used for illegal purposes"[3] (cash is also non traceable and used more frequently by criminals), and so on and so forth.

The important point to bear in mind is that everything works in cycles, and people's sentiments usually follow suit. Understandably, there's still a lot of bearishness and skepticism in the market. That might have turned around by the time you're reading this, or maybe not. Either way, it doesn't matter much, when there's green on a chart people are happy and when there's red they're sad. When the price is going up, everyone is cheery and the media is making wild predictions one way; when the price is down people are making predictions the other way (it's going down!). It's like a yo-yo with the string being investor emotions—we've all gotten caught up in it.

BULLISH ON BITCOIN

There a lot of positive stories you don't hear about in the media. Take, for instance, the Afghani girl who lives in a country where women typically aren't allowed to have bank accounts (their brothers/fathers control the accounts). By using bitcoin she's able to gain a level of not only financial freedom, but also personal freedom that literally transforms her life.

Or the Filipino who sends money back home, but is milked by disgustingly high fees by Western Union; switching to Bitcoin Cash

---

2 Andreas M. Antonopoulos, "Energy Consumption and Bitcoin," Youtube video, https://m.youtube.com/watch?v=2T0OUIW89II.
3 Andreas M. Antonopoulos, "Bitcoin and Crime," Youtube video, https://m.youtube.com/watch?v=dZ1_2aJKY-U.

INTRODUCTION

saves his family thousands per year, a considerable sum for those in developing countries.

There are many benefits for the developed world, too. Americans paid over 15 BILLION dollars—that's 15,000,000,000—just in overdraft fees to banks last year. These are the same banks who spurred the latest financial crisis and then just months later shamelessly cut multi-million dollar bonus paychecks (Goldman Sachs...) while Americans lost their jobs and homes.[4]

You cannot transform the entire world without some pushback, and you certainly can't do it in just 10 years. Maybe 20, 30 or 50 years. Because blockchain is inherently disruptive, it requires a lot of infrastructure to work properly. It's not compatible with short-term gains. Fortunately, there is a lot of institutional infrastructure being built that will support the ecosystem.

The fact that people lost money and we haven't solved all the issues shouldn't be cause for defeat. In the background, thousands of people are working hard at solving these challenges. The problems of scalability, utility and stability need to be addressed. And they are being tackled every day by people who have dedicated their lives to doing so. The vision is still alive. But altruism is not the only motivation; the financial incentives are still there.

Overall, I see it as *good* news that we haven't figured it out. It means that there is plenty of opportunity for people to come in and create. It's not too late to build something great and make lots of money in the process. To build new products that nobody's ever heard of; to create the next

---

4 Richard Wachmn and Phillip Inman, "Goldman Bonuses," *The Guardian*, https://www.theguardian.com/business/2009/dec/06/goldman-bankers-bonus-recovery.

Facebook that looks nothing like Facebook. Who will be the Google of the crypto space? We don't know, and that's an exciting thought.

For a trader or investor, traditional methods and valuation frameworks don't work in cryptocurrencies. They're still too new. Price discovery is still necessary to find the "true" value of many of these currencies. This uncertainty gives you a chance to find your own edge. There are dozens of methods that haven't been thought of. The ambitious and driven and dreamers among us have a choice. We can be part of it, or we can stand on the sidelines and watch the world change. The genie has been let out of the bottle and—call me an optimist—I'm bullish.

BAPTISM BY FIRE

When I first heard about bitcoin—I think I read an article online somewhere—my curiosity was immediately piqued. Deciding that this was worth 10 minutes of my time, I started reading a few more articles. *Huh, what's all this bitcoin stuff about?*

A few minutes passed. I was trying to wrap my head around the technology and its implications for the financial industry, and society as a whole. *Holy shit.* Something clicked, and I could see a whole new world unfolding before me. Spurred by a growing desire to learn more, I cancelled all my meetings for the day.

'Sorry, something urgent came up, and I can't do anything or go anywhere today.'

I set all of my responsibilities aside and brewed a giant pot of coffee. I was going to need it. I furiously consumed every piece of content about bitcoin that I could get my hands on. I read through Satoshi's white paper, the ethereum white paper, a handful of books and the

INTRODUCTION

million resources on Jameson Lopp's site.[5] I absorbed everything I could until my eyes were red and my girlfriend reminded me to eat. This was my starting point on a journey that continues to this day.

Like many, I quickly realized that I knew little about the history of money. Where do you start and where do you end? Now I had to read about the Medicis, Keynesian and Austrian economics, and then the history of the internet and network theory and...There was so much to know, and so much I was (and still am) ignorant about. The one day turned into one week, and the one week turned into two years.

What if we could build a company with no bosses? A company that managed itself, that had the rules written into its code? And what if this company could build great things using algorithms that talked to themselves? That's the DAO—Decentralized Autonomous Organization. What if we lived in a world where you had full control of your money? A currency that was not inflationary? And where the government couldn't take away your money? That's the bitcoin value proposition. What if we could get paid every 2 seconds instead of every two weeks? Smart contracts can do that.[6]

The best way to get to know something is to get your hands dirty. So, I opened an account on a large exchange here in Japan where I live. I made my first purchase and then found myself interested in trading. This was in 2016 before all the mania struck.

I jumped into the rabbit hole, and have since invested countless hours reading dense white papers, learning technical analysis and

---

5 Jameson Lopp, *Bitcoin Resources*, https://lopp.net/bitcoin.html.
6 Granted, there are still shortcomings. The $50 million DAO hack, high transaction fees, and volatile nature of cryptocurrencies show us that all of these propositions are still a work in progress.

grasping the mechanics of market psychology. In the process I made all of the classic mistakes—I blindly followed certain traders, fell for scams, and didn't sell when I was profiting, greedily hoping the price would rise infinitely to the moon. My mistakes cost me a lot.

Ultimately these mishaps pushed me towards painful self-reflection and led me to join a community where I could receive feedback and learn from people more experienced than myself. My biggest breakthrough came when I was able to approach the market with a sense of equanimity—that is, staying level-headed and not responding to fluctuations emotionally. I'm still learning every day. I've switched my focus from actively "day trading" (a losing strategy) to making smarter, longer-term investments. Now I spend my time researching and writing long-form articles about crypto, as well deploying marketing strategies for startups in the blockchain space, continually fascinated by the new world we're building.

THE PROVERBIAL RABBIT HOLE

> *"Momentum begets momentum, and the best way to start is to start."*
> —GIL PENCHINA

Why do people get sucked down the rabbit hole? Why have people quit their high paying jobs to jump into an industry that hasn't proven any viable business model on a large scale (at least not yet)?

Crypto is attractive to creative people who like revolutionary ideas; it requires you to have an understanding of technology, economics, psychology and history. In fact, you simply *can't* understand it unless you take a multidisciplinary approach. You have to question your assumptions that teachers, parents and society have ingrained in you all these years.

The good news is you don't have to be a technical expert or some guru analyst to make money. Nor do you have to grasp every single aspect of blockchain to make decent earnings or generate a passive income. You certainly don't have to be sitting in front of your computer every day and trading; most day traders lose money daily, anyways. You can make money and still have a life.

So if you're at the start of your journey, welcome. Now take a leap forward. I recommend you jump headfirst into the rabbit hole. This may take you a few hours, days or weeks. Once you emerge, come back to this book. Much of what I write about will be more useful if you've actually used crypto in your life (trading, investing) and have a fundamental understanding of the various value propositions of cryptocurrencies. So, if you haven't, go do the following right away:

1. Open an account on a crypto exchange in your country. Big ones include Bittrex, Bitfinex, and Coinbase.
2. Buy your first cryptocurrency.
3. Watch at least five hours of videos on Andreas Antonopoulos's Youtube channel: https://www.youtube.com/user/aantonop/featured

WHAT YOU'LL GET FROM THIS BOOK

Many people I know have been trading cryptocurrencies since 2013, so my three years of trading and investing may seem short in comparison. However, I've face-planted many times along the way, and have learned how to face-plant less. My hope is that at least some of my lessons-learned will be valuable to others. I've also interviewed, spoken to and gathered insights from dozens of professional traders, investors and blockchain experts. I have written this book to share these successful cryptocurrency and trading strategies with you.

Part one discusses trading strategy. Research has shown that day traders lose money over the long run; even the most technically savvy traders lose because of psychological pressure (theory is much harder in practice when you're on the battlefield) and failing to manage risk. Thus, I largely focus on mental fortitude, risk management and creating profitable systems. This book is not very technical—it's a mix of specific tactics to make money and how to not *lose* money. That said there are some charts and graphs, so if you're not interested in trading, you can skip to part two and three.

Part two delves into over 37 strategies that you can put to use today. It's a mix of trading, marketing, and technology-related techniques. My goal is that it will open you up to what investment opportunities are possible. Some you have heard of, others might be new, but all are generally accessible to anybody with an internet connection.

Part three explores investing with longer-term horizons in mind. How do you assess a specific crypto asset? What metrics do successful investors use to look at crypto projects? What are the most interesting projects in crypto right now and what should we look out for? For those interested in starting a career in blockchain, you will find the tips from startup founders useful.

I suppose I should write a disclaimer here. You *can* lose all of your money. That's the whole "high-risk high reward" thing. So, don't listen to me. And don't follow anything I do on blind faith. Do your own digging and find out what's right for you. Everyone has a different tolerance for risk. Also, technology changes rapidly. I know that some methods will become outdated quickly, and I will do my best to keep the information updated. If you feel that I have missed something, feel free to reach out to me at newcryptoeconomy@gmail.com.

PART 1
TRADING

Chapter 1

KNOW THYSELF

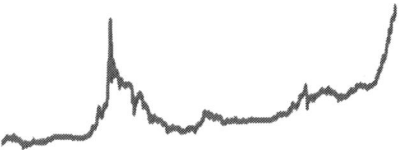

"It is not enough only to be a student at the beginning. It is a position that one has to assume for life. Learn from everyone and everything. From the people you beat, and the people who beat you, from the people you dislike, even from your supposed enemies. At every step and every juncture in life, there is the opportunity to learn and even if the lesson is purely remedial, we must not let ego block us from hearing it again."
—RYAN HOLIDAY, EGO IS THE ENEMY

INVESTING VS. TRADING VS. SPECULATING

In a little known story, Sir Isaac Newton bought some stocks of the South Sea Company, a British trading company popular back in the 1700s. He sold the shares for a nice profit, but shortly after he got greedy and swept up in the exuberance of the times. He bought back the stock at a much higher price. Unfortunately, he lost almost all of it—equivalent to millions of dollars in today's money. The great physicist "could calculate the motions of the heavenly bodies, but not the madness of the people."[7]

You could classify Newton's general activity as "investing," but what he was really doing was trading—buying stocks at an opportunistic market price and expecting to sell for a profit in a relatively short amount of time. You could further say that he was a speculator. When the price increased dramatically, although "what goes up must come down," he rolled the die. Unlike, say a gold miner hedging the potential change in price of a gold shipment on a South Sea voyage, a speculator does not own the underlying assets. Although speculation is often used interchangeably with trading, generally speculation implies a much higher risk-reward ratio more in line with borderline gambling (if not synonymous with gambling).

For simplicity I'm going to lump trading and speculating into the same category, and investing in its own category. There are a few key differences between investors and traders. Traders usually think in terms of shorter time frames and bet on market fluctuations to make a profit. Investors are less susceptible to the ups and downs of the market, preferring to look at longer time horizons. These HODLRs are more likely to do a fundamental analysis of the company/project, rather than purely a technical analysis of a chart. The long-term investor is willing to take temporary drawdowns on their account (aka, lose money) that would make the average trader curl up in the fetal position.

There are opportunities, particularly in very volatile markets like crypto, to profit from both approaches. For example, when a coin

---

7 Elena Holodny, "Sir Isaac Newton Lost a Fortune," *Business Insider*, https://www.businessinsider.com/isaac-newton-lost-a-fortune-on-englands-hottest-stock-2016-1

capitulates (when the price drops drastically) and the market is in utter despair, a savvy trader will come in and buy at dirt cheap prices, even though it's psychologically paralyzing to buy when there's so much red on the screen—in other words, striking while the iron is hot. An investor doesn't even pay attention to daily, weekly or even monthly fluctuations in price, instead choosing to look at the bigger picture.

In the seminal book *The Intelligent Investor,* Benjamin Graham reminds us that it is possible to be both an intelligent trader *and* an intelligent investor.

Here are three common ways trading can be *un*intelligent:

1. You're trading when you think you're investing.
2. You trade full time (instead of approaching it as a pastime) without having the knowledge and skill for it.
3. You risk more money than you can afford to lose.

The intelligent investor will, first and foremost, differentiate between both types of activities. Then, they'll consider all of the factors that might affect both strategies. One of my biggest mistakes has been confusing the two, and then getting upset when I lost money on a trade. Upon further reflection, I was treating a trade as if it were an investment.

Hodling is an investment strategy that has psychologically sabotaged itself. While people say they are "holding for the long term," they continue to check daily price actions, as if they were trading, when in reality they should ignore daily fluctuation. When you are constantly concerned with short-term price but refuse to sell, you begin to confuse your investment with a trade.

Ask yourself the following questions:

- *Am I investing for the short term or long term?* If the answer is short, you're trading. If the answer is long, you're investing.
- *Why am I making this investment or trade?* If you're buying a token[8] simply because the price is low, you're looking solely at the market and making a trade. Taking a more holistic approach and assessing the long-term viability of the project is an investment.
- *Would I make the same decision again given the information I have, even if I lost money?* You can lose money on individual trades as long as some of them are winning trades—no trader is perfect. Focus on the process.
- *What are the tax advantages or disadvantages of a particular investment or trade?* Taxes can bite you in the short term if you sell too soon. Factor in the real cost of making a trade.

THE ACTIVE VS. PASSIVE APPROACH

What kind of trader or investor are you? The active investor takes a hands-on approach to seeking out knowledge and is constantly on the forefront of new investments. This is intellectually stimulating but also time consuming. It means reading lots of white papers, always looking for an "edge" and experimenting with new ways to make money. The passive investor doesn't want to deal with all the

---

[8] There are two types of tokens: utility tokens and security tokens. Utility tokens are a non-physical token, or "digital coupons," issued to fund development of, and later buy products and services from, a service. They are what ICOs were issuing to hopeful investors and the object of much speculation. Security tokens, on the other hand, derive their value from an external, tradable asset, including real physical companies, real estate, or an entitlement to dividends or interest payments. Security tokens are analogous to equities, bonds or derivatives.

CHAPTER 1. KNOW THYSELF

fuss; they want to spend as little time as possible and manage their investments on autopilot. They don't like to think about money.

Many investors will find that they fall somewhere in between. They have full-time jobs and can't dedicate every waking moment to investing, but they don't want to passively leave their returns in the hands of an investment manager or a robo-advisor. They want a balanced portfolio and occasionally enjoy taking a more active role in managing their own portfolio. I've invested in gold, for example, which is a low-maintenance investment; I don't need to think about this (and so, it's kind of a boring investment). On the other hand, marijuana stocks are newer (with perhaps magic mushroom stocks soon to come!9), and therefore I have to keep a closer eye on the market. I love researching new projects; I like to dig deep into the mechanics and imagine a world where that technology comes to fruition.

Neither approach is better than the other, and you can do very well with both. The key is knowing what kind of investor you are. Financial risk is half about the investment and half about ourselves; *can we manage our own emotions amidst uncertainty?* Those more prone to emotional decision-making are better off starting with more passive trading and investing strategies in order to minimize risk; as you hone your skills and mental/emotional fortitude, you can dip your toes in the water and take a more active approach.

With experience, traders rely less on intuitive 'emotional' responses and more on rational thinking based on learned knowledge. Your ancient reptilian brain, for example, would be activated at the zoo when you see a jaguar within a glass enclosure. When the jaguar takes

---

9 Lilly Dancyger, "Oregon is Considering Legalizing Psilocybin Mushrooms in 2020," *Rolling Stone*, https://bit.ly/2RzLb6T.

PART 1. TRADING

a swipe at you, the primitive part of your brain reacts with fear and flight. It's only later that the more evolved part of your brain introduces logic: "There's a sheet of glass between myself and the predator. I have never been attacked at a zoo. I do not know anyone who has been attacked by an animal at a zoo (learned knowledge!). Therefore, I'm safe." A fear reaction is not indicated.

Our primitive brain urged us to run, as natural selection requiring no conscious thought favors these sorts of "false positives." From this evolutionary perspective, we are primed to react on the basis of emotion, but more likely to make errors. If applying logic, on the other hand, it takes a concerted effort to develop the mental fortitude you need to be a disciplined trader. Simulated trading and backtesting are required to test your strategies and learn more about how they will perform.

Trading as a more active endeavor is more likely to elicit emotional responses. You need to watch the market, set alerts, and make moves at the right times depending on your profit targets. Investing is lower maintenance and requires more of a check-up on the current state of the project and company. Your approach will change depending on where you're at in your life. This will also determine how much time you're willing to commit, and the amount of risk capital (money) you're willing to put towards your investments. Start by considering the factors that affect your risk profile and plan accordingly to determine which investment strategy suits you.

- *Given your salary and monthly expenditures, how much are you willing to lose every month?*
- *Do you have emergency cash in case you lose your job?*
- *If you own a business or work for yourself, how much cash flow do you need to survive for six months? What about one year?*

CHAPTER 1. KNOW THYSELF

- *What other financial commitments will you have over the next 1–3 years (marriage/car/house/travel/kids/taxes)?*

Most people take too much risk because they don't plan. If you want to take a more active approach to crypto, answer the above questions honestly and determine how much money you realistically have available to risk each month. Once you've got a number, say, $500 every month (this is called dollar-cost averaging), don't diverge from your plan.[10]

As a trader that means you'll take $500 from your income and put it into your trading account, and not a cent more. Never mix your risk capital account (money you have on an exchange, for example) with money you need for groceries; otherwise, you will set yourself up for potentially bad decision-making. Reassess these factors at least once a quarter. For investors who have a chunk of cash available and prefer to make a larger one-off investment and be done with it, we'll cover this option in Part III.

YOUR THREE BUCKETS

I've had friends who bought Bitcoin for the "long term" but then sold it after a few months at a loss. Others "trading" cryptocurrencies *hodl* their dear coins when the price drops in hopes of mega-gains sometime in the future. Failing to cut your losses and move on is well known to be the major reason traders lose money. Others set up for a big swing trade over weeks or months, but cut out because they read a negative *Huffpost* article that convinced them crypto was a fad.

The importance of mental and emotional fortitude and resilience is nothing new in the world of trading, but it becomes ever more crucial

---

10 Check glossary of terms for more on *dollar-cost averaging*.

PART 1. TRADING

in our digital environment. We've become increasingly less patient, more anxious, more distracted, and more easily swayed than we've ever been[11]. We live in a world where saying "you have the attention span of a goldfish" has actually become a compliment (the average attention span has dropped down to 8 seconds—less than a goldfish). The Coinmarketcap app certainly helps in fueling our addiction.

I've made these mistakes, too. Fortunately, I never borrowed money, unlike some of the poor guys mentioned in the sobering *NY Times* piece about the post-crypto boom[12]. Those most easily swayed by the waves of irrational exuberance are those that go in with zero plan. They buy bitcoin or altcoins in reaction (emotionally) to a tweet, a reddit post, an article they've read, or advice from a friend. But in doing so, they throw their plans out the window, and risk management goes with it. *Splat.* Considering that money is on the line, this is often disastrous.

Nobody is going to protect you, so you best heed these three basic rules of investing money in crypto and surviving the shark-infested waters.

1. *Have a plan.* When you invest, decide what type of investment you're making (see below).
2. *Diversify.* Don't put all your cash or crypto in one exchange. Split it up into several exchanges. Buy two hardware Trezor (or Ledger

---

[11] "Greater use of media is correlated with higher levels of trait impulsivity and distractibility, but the direction of causality has not been established. Individuals may become more skilled at media multitasking over time, but intervention is currently required to improve the safe and effective use of mobile media." Laura E. Levine, "Mobile Media Use, Multitasking and Distractibility," *International Journal of Cyber Behavior, Psychology and Learning*, https://www.igi-global.com/article/content/70087.

[12] Nathaniel Popper and Su-Hyun Lee, "After the Bitcoin Boom," *NYTimes*, https://www.nytimes.com/2018/08/20/technology/cryptocurrency-investor-losses.html.

CHAPTER 1. KNOW THYSELF

Nano S) wallets, and keep one at your parents house and bury one in your backyard just in case.

3. *Don't make investment decisions when you've had too many Mojitos.* You'll almost always regret it. (In other words, when you're physical or emotional state is clouded, don't make important decisions)[13]

THREE CAPITAL BUCKETS FOR CRYPTO

I'm assuming you'll want to mix trading and investing, and play around with other crypto-generating strategies. Using buckets will help you follow rule two, Diversify, by allocating your investments across different time horizons and verticals.

Make the mental distinction between the following three investment allocations and plan your investments accordingly.

1. *Short-term trading capital mostly in fiat currency or stablecoins (days/weeks/months).* You want to have ammunition in the form of USD/GBP/YEN, ready to buy. Never use 100% of the cash because you will always benefit from having the dry powder. What if bitcoin goes down to $1,000 tomorrow? You want extra cash set aside to be able to scoop some up. Here I'm looking for short-term gains of 30%+.
2. *Long-term investment capital (multi-year holds, pre-ICOs, STOs).* Put these long-term investments in cold storage and don't touch them for a couple of years. You should NOT be checking the price on these regularly. Check in every few weeks/months. If you're planning to sell some of these if they go to say, 10x or 20x, then you can set price alerts via email.

---

13 If we look at this from a neuroscientific perspective, you're hijacking/paralyzing the higher road/rational thinking capacities of your brain in the same way that gambling would.

3. *Passive income buckets/miscellaneous (trading bots/masternodes/airdrops/dividends/affiliate income).* There are so many ways to make a little bit of extra money with crypto now that it's hard to keep track of them. You can treat these investments as short-long term—it's up to you (for example, use the LTC trading bot to make 1.4% returns/day and either pull it out after a few weeks or reinvest your earnings for a few months.)

Let's say you have $5,000 USD. If you were to put all of that into one trade without any stop-loss orders, the next day you could wake up to a burned out red candle and 50% of your portfolio wiped out. The game can be over quickly.

Everybody's penchant for risk is different, so I can't say what's right for you. The best solution for each individual depends on so many factors. But I'd say it's more sensible to take that 5k and put 2-3k of it into longer term and passive income streams and keep 2k in cash for your ammunition to trade and buy dips.

Whatever ratio you decide on, be crystal clear about which bucket it's going into. This will reduce your stress, improve your focus, and save you from panic trading. Decide which buckets you're going to use and stick to your plan.

THE FIVE TRUTHS OF TRADING CRYPTOCURRENCIES

There are definitely more truths of trading, but here are the recurring ones that have found to be the cause of much unnecessary anguish.

1. With great volatility comes great opportunity

The more volatility the better. When I hear the news about the stock market going up or down fractions of a point, I think, *What? That's tiny*. I don't think I could ever trade stocks, at least not in the short term. Everybody has a different penchant for risk. Some people experience a gut-wrenching feeling when they see the price fluctuations in cryptocurrencies. I get excited! They see price drops of 40% and they see blood. On the other side of the screen, an 18-year-old kid in Seoul is taking full of advantage of the situation and shorting the market.

2. People fear what they don't understand. So, aim to understand more than most people.
It's easy to be a skeptic, it's easy to be afraid. It's also easy to shoot darts blindfolded, buy a bunch of random coins (spray and pray), and hope for the best. Time is limited and we can't spend days and weeks researching one project. There is an opportunity cost to waiting, and no action is still an action.

A little research goes a long way, though. If you don't understand something, ask on a forum, watch videos, or post your question on Quora. Talk to people who are more educated than you and get your information from various sources. No trader is going to make money on every trade, nor is an investor going to make money on every investment. It's called high risk, high reward for a reason.

However, we can control certain things. We can perform our due diligence, establish processes, and minimize risk. We can ignore social media frenzy and hype on the news, and instead come to our own educated conclusions. Even if we are wrong and ultimately don't make money on X trade or X investment, we should be confident in saying that "I would do that again given the information I had." That's the best we can strive for.

3. Everything goes in cycles.

I would put this on a billboard if I could. People tell me they saw that X regulation was rejected, or they read some negative article about bitcoin. They ask me if they should buy or sell their bitcoin. When this happens I get a little frustrated. I can't make that decision for them. Their lack of direction also indicates that they have no plan. My response is usually along these lines. "I don't know, but the market goes in cycles. Oh, and is it money you're willing to lose?" If they are not willing to lose it, they should have it in cash, not something that could disappear tomorrow. Sure, the banks could shut down—I know. So diversify.

When bitcoin hit 20k it was a "new paradigm." People were saying it would go to 50k or 1 million a coin. Maybe one day, but nothing keeps going up and up forever. When the price started to drop from 20k, people were in denial. *"Yeh, it'll go back up. Just wait!"* Of course, as we know, it didn't. Smart traders shorted and were not surprised. Dumb money bought high and sold low.

Nobody can predict the highs or the lows of the market, but we can predict that there will be a high and low, because that's how all markets work. Bitcoin has faced several historical corrections over the past few years, some bloodier than others, but not unlike what we're seeing now.

CHAPTER 1. KNOW THYSELF

Bitcoin Historical Price Corrections List of bitcoins major corrections >30% (from ATH levels) since January 2012						
Correction Start Date (d/m/y)	Correction End Date	# Days in Correction	Bitcoin High Price	Bitcoin Low Price	% Decline	$ Decline
1/12/2012	1/27/2012	16	$7.38	$3.80	-49%	-$3.58
8/17/2012	8/19/2012	3	$16.41	$7.10	-57%	-$9.31
03/06/2013	03/07/2013	2	$49.17	$33.00	-33%	-$16.17
03/21/2013	03/23/2013	3	$76.91	$50.09	-35%	-$26.82
04/10/2013	04/12/2013	3	$259.34	$45.00	-83%	-$214.34
11/19/2013	11/19/2013	1	$755	$378.00	-50%	-$377.00
11/30/2013	01/14/2015	411	$1,163	$152.40	-87%	-$1,1010.6
03/10/2017	03/25/2017	16	$1,1350	$891.33	-34%	-$458.67
05/25/2017	05/27/2017	3	$2,760	$1,850	-33%	-$910.10
06/12/2017	07/16/2017	35	$2,980	$1,830	-39%	-$1,150
09/2/2017	09/15/2017	14	$4,979	$2,972.01	-40%	-$2,007.89
11/08/2017	11/12/2017	5	$7,888	$5,555.55	-30%	-$2,332.45
12/17/2017	12/19/2018	337	$19,666	$5,187.12	-74%	-$14,478

There are coins which have lost 95% of their value within a few days. If that scares you, then you shouldn't invest money you can't afford to lose. So, we don't know what the bottom price of bitcoin could be. Maybe it's 6k, 5k, 1k or lower. But one thing we can say: the longer bitcoin is around, the longer it is likely to be around (coined "the Lindy Effect" by Nassim Taleb)[14]

4. Cash is king

It doesn't matter how bullish you are—if you have all of your money in crypto, sure, you can always shop online until more merchants accept crypto, but your life is not measured by the amount of dogecoin you have. To avoid being destroyed, don't put all your money into

---

[14] Nassim Nicholas Taleb, "The Black Swan," (New York: Random House, 2007).

crypto. One risk is hard-to-predict Black Swan events, like exchanges getting hacked, new regulations, whales taking dumps on the market. Join an investment group in which people hold you accountable. An underestimated risk is your own ego. The market does not care about whether you're right. It will give you no insurance and will chew you up and spit you out. To avoid the treacherous jaws of the market you have to play it smart, and that means always having cash on hand. Cash will remain king (and maybe stablecoins).

5. Diversify or die

When I travel I keep two copies of my passport; one at the hotel and one on me. I don't take all my bank cards or credit cards with me. What if I get robbed? I also don't keep all my money on one exchange, or on one Trezor, or even in one country. I don't keep it all in cryptocurrencies. The average millionaire has seven bank accounts and seven streams of income. Don't think about only diversifying amongst different cryptocurrencies, but more generally, how to hedge your risk in every way possible.

Chapter 2

THE ONLY TRADING STRATEGY YOU WILL EVER NEED

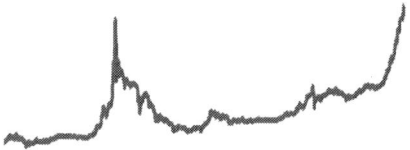

*It is easy in the world to live after the world's opinion;
it is easy in solitude to live after our own; but the great man
is he who in the midst of the crowd keeps with perfect
sweetness the independence of solitude.*
—RALPH WALDO EMERSON

Most new investors become dizzy when faced with choosing from dozens of charting tools to view the market. You could spend days analyzing one coin and convince yourself that the price is going to go up tomorrow. And when it does, you'll convince yourself that your method is the best. It works, until it doesn't.

I'm assuming you've already done a bit of research on trading. Or that you've traded a bit yourself. I'm a very simple trader. I don't like to analyze charts beyond what is absolutely necessary, and I do so mainly to manage risk and understand my risk-reward ratio. I don't pretend I can predict the future.

Traders who already know the basics might want to…still read this part. I'm outlining what I find to be the most fundamental, important skills in trading, which have less to do with technical analysis and more to do with managing yourself. It's a simple plan, but it works.

THE FOUR STEPS OF A TRADE SETUP

"I will prepare and some day my chance will come."
—ABRAHAM LINCOLN

Let's take a look at four ways to conduct an analysis before executing a trade, regardless of whether it's a short- or long-term investment.

- Fundamental Analysis
- Technical Analysis (TA)
- Market Sentiment Analysis
- Self-Analysis

The highly optimistic and impulsive trader by nature might research a project like Cardano (ADA) and conclude that it is undervalued. Trigger happy, he sees the price rising and jumps to buy without creating a plan. He ignores important factors like its correlation to bitcoin, the current market sentiment, and its market capitalization— all factors that could be relevant to his trading strategy. His recent successful trade has left him feeling lucky, so he is more likely to act on emotion. Sometimes we'll get lucky, other times we won't.

All four types of analyses could help instill discipline in this emotion-driven trader. We all have strengths and weaknesses. Some may gravitate towards the bigger picture, like market/fundamental analysis, while others will be more drawn to the TA. You might even feel like you have an edge over others because of a particular strength you have. Good. But simply picking and choosing only *one* of the above strategies you like or are skilled at leaves you susceptible to gaping blind spots. The point: We can still maintain our edge using our strengths, but we can't totally ignore the other factors!

#1 Fundamental Analysis

Fundamental analysis involves conducting research on the viability of the project, engagement of their community (on Slack/telegram/discord/etc.), adherence to a development schedule (perhaps on Github), white paper, and team. Like an angel investment, you're trying to measure the intrinsic value of something that has a statistically high chance of going bust.

Fundamental analysis matters less when you're trading because you're looking at the shorter term. When it comes to **trading**, I spend at most 2-3 hours on fundamental analysis—sometimes I spend no time at all. I'll also ask people I trust what their thoughts on X project are, and add that into my mix of considerations, keeping in mind that everyone has their own view.

When it comes to **investing** for the longer term, fundamental analysis is a lot more important. Let's take the BABB project for example, which is a centralized blockchain-based 'bank account' based out of London. Cool concept. Though, if you're to compare the team to an "all-star" one like *Beetoken's*, you might decide to not invest in BABB purely on this basis—or at least mark them down a couple of points in your mind.

In reality, both are great *long-term* holds, but whether or not you should trade them has almost nothing to do with how great their

PART 1. TRADING

teams or projects are. When BABB had their ICO, the token started trading at around triple the ICO price.[15] Some might think that's not very much. It's funny because the crypto markets are the only markets in the world where you can feel salty and bitter because you doubled or tripled your money, but didn't 10x it. Kind of crazy isn't it?

My point is that while fundamental analysis is certainly important, you can still get a winning coin and make a profit even if the project doesn't rate 5 out of 5 stars. When you're in a bull market, almost everything goes up, and you should care less about the project as a whole and more about being smart about taking profit and cashing out before the price plummets.

#2 Technical Analysis–Beware of Analysis Paralysis

Whether you're trading cryptocurrencies frequently or investing in blockchain projects for the long term, once you get the fundamentals of buying/selling, it's really not that complicated.

I remember reading a 90-page PDF about the history,[16] theory and practical applications of using the Fibonacci sequence—the famous mathematical pattern appearing throughout nature in which each number is the sum of the two previous numbers. Many traders consider it an important tool to have in the toolshed. I was able to learn the practical application of this technical trading tool in 20 minutes from a YouTube video and then by observing other traders.

Day traders spend an inordinate amount of time looking at charts, checking their phones and trying to make small gains here and there.

---

15 "BABB ICO," *ICODrops*, https://icodrops.com/babb/.
16 Wayne Gorman, "How Can You Identify Turning Points Using Fibonacci," https://www.amazon.com/Identify-Turning-Points-Using-Fibonacci-ebook/dp/B001XURBC6.

This preoccupation leads to over-complicating things, not to mention an unhealthy lifestyle. There's been at least one story of a bitcoin investor who committed suicide.[17]

Of course, having a basic grasp of technical analysis is still important (H&S, flags, wedges etc.). You can analyze the crap out of a chart, draw a million lines on it and make it say whatever you want it to say. You can run Fibonacci extensions a dozen ways, stare at logarithmic scales and convince yourself that a certain coin is going to the moon sometime in the not-to-distant future.

Like using KPIs in the business world, technical analysis is largely comprised of *indicators,* not ultimate truths. Forecasting is as much of a science as it is an art. Especially in retrospect, when a coin does well, you can use this to justify your superb technical skills.

The best traders I have spoken to might only execute a couple of trades per month and are extremely selective about setting up trades. Rather than trying to catch each tiny ripple (no pun intended), they focus on catching the big waves.

The hardest part about all of this is not analyzing charts, it's *over-analyzing* them, as this can lead to over-trading and regrets. There are so many examples of crypto traders who could have done nothing and made significantly larger gains (like the million-dollar trading mistake)[18]. In other words, after you learn the basics, keep things simple with the charts.

---

17 Cy Mukherjee, "How Bitcoin Can Take Its Toll on Your Mental Health," *Fortune,* http://fortune.com/2017/12/08/bitcoin-investing-mental-health/.
18 Edward T. Giraffe, "Hackernoon: Million Dollar Trading Mistakes," *Hackernoon,* https://hackernoon.com/million-dollar-trading-mistakes-for-your-entertainment-and-edification-e9bbf9675a8b.

#3 Market Sentiment—"The Trend Is Your Friend"

> "You want to be greedy when others are fearful. You want to be fearful when others are greedy. It's that simple."
> —WARREN BUFFETT, FOUNDER OF BERKSHIRE HATHAWAY

It's easy to get caught up listening to people who think their coin is the Yahoo! of the crypto economy, and are willing to go to great lengths to prove their loyalty. It's also tempting to follow the coins they're shilling on Twitter.

The wave of bitcoin maximalists who support the libertarian dream say "HODL your shitcoins because the price *will* go up," as if they have a crystal ball. Over the long run, they may be right. In fact, I'm very bullish on a lot of projects myself, especially when it comes to 2–5 year timeframes.

However, many people enter the market as traders looking to make shorter to mid-term gains. Many are trying to pay the bills, in which case infinite gains and hope are not good strategies.

> "Never ask anyone for their opinion, forecast, or recommendation. Just ask them what they have—or don't have—in their portfolio."
> —NASSIM NICHOLAS TALEB, ANTIFRAGILE: THINGS THAT GAIN FROM DISORDER

All markets follow cycles. Whether that's bitcoin, stocks, oil, tulips, real estate—you name it.

CHAPTER 2. THE ONLY TRADING STRATEGY YOU WILL EVER NEED

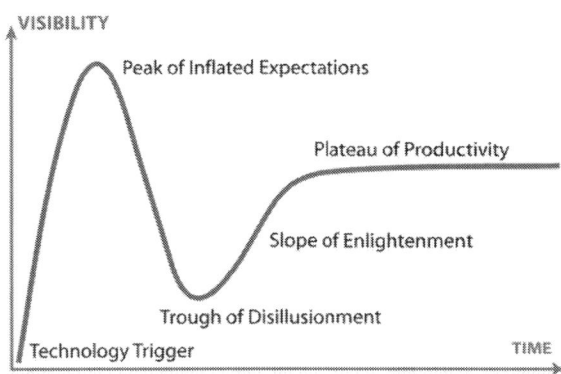

Ignoring market cycles results in grabbing whatever coin appears shiniest and then watching the price plummet—forcing you to "bag hold"—holding onto those precious coins with dear life in the hopes that they will go up in value. I made this mistake, too.

This hysteria was at its worst (so far, but will undoubtedly repeat) back in December/January 2017 (and who knows, it might happen again). The media entered the picture, we had mass euphoria (bitcoin to 100k!), and everybody was buying bitcoin at 20k before it crashed.

The best traders I know look at the larger market cycles, gauge market sentiment, and do the opposite of whatever CNBC is saying you should do.

Don't mistake a *"cyclical trend"* for an *"infinite direction."*

PART 1. TRADING

#4 Self Analysis—I am my own boss

There are two steps to this process. 1) Making a plan. 2) Checking-in with yourself every week.

1) Make a Plan, Stick With It

At one point I blindly followed a couple of traders whom I respected. A coin they had suggested to buy absolutely tanked and it really ticked me off because I had chosen to follow their advice. Of course, I had no right to be upset. It was totally my decision and responsibility—only I was to blame.

It takes a lot more discipline, time and effort to make your own plan. This is also scarier because it means that you're ultimately accountable for both your gains *and* your losses.

I suggest keeping a trading journal wherein you can specify your reasons for entering the trade, define profit targets, and answer difficult questions like, "If the price of this goes down by 90%, what action will I take?"

Remember that 'success' can mean different things to different people, but we have to define it and manage our own risks. What is *your* definition of success?

The saying in crypto goes, "I was a millionaire in January and broke in February!"

Another big mistake I made was trying to mold my own goals to the behaviors of the market. The problem is, the market doesn't give a hoot about your financial goals. I've found it's better to not set monetary goals in terms of a specific $ amount, but instead, base them on percentages ("take 30% of my profit from the position").

CHAPTER 2. THE ONLY TRADING STRATEGY YOU WILL EVER NEED

We have to think in terms of probabilities, not in terms of exact, *definite* outcomes that are simply impossible to predict—that's called "predicting the future." Your predefined risk limits will help to identify your profit taking percentages. Measuring your risk-reward ratio before every trade is an important risk management step.

Rather than fixating on a specific figure and timeline, a more valuable use of time would be to focus on building skills that will increase the probability of the outcome you desire. Consistency and discipline will result in profits down the line.

2) Weekly Performance Review

> *"Success consists of going from failure to failure without loss of enthusiasm."*
> —WINSTON CHURCHILL

When you don't have a boss looking over your shoulder or giving you a quarterly performance review, it can be difficult to measure your progress. Y*ou're* responsible for your own assessment. This is both a blessing and a curse because it allows you ultimate freedom but also ultimate responsibility.

The weekly self-check is a good practice to adopt. Ask yourself the following questions:

- *Did I stick with my plan in my trading journal?* Track your trades in an Excel document—include entry/exit targets, reasons for buying, and profit targets. Review them and be honest with yourself, but don't beat yourself up if you missed targets. There's always the next trade.

- *How do I feel?* Have I given myself time to develop mental/emotional strength? As discussed in the first section, make sure you're taking time to stay healthy.
- *What did I learn?* What did you learn (Did you make a trade you regret?) and how will you correct for it in the future? (For example, I would frequently check the price of a coin but now I use price alerts, and stop loss and limit orders, which give me a lot more room to breathe).

Get into a habit of using these four tools—they could save you a lot of time and money. Ultimately, black swan events like new government regulations or founders running off with money could negate any of your analyses, so keep in mind that regardless of your investment it's always vital to manage for downside risk—that is, don't put all your chips on the table in case you're wiped out.

POSITION SIZING

The size of a position within a particular portfolio, or the dollar amount that an investor is going to trade. Investors use position sizing to help determine how many units of a security they can purchase, which helps them to control risk and maximize returns.

Setting Stop Losses

How much are you willing to risk per trade? Generally speaking, unless it's a long-term investment, you shouldn't be risking very much per trade. Professional traders and money managers recommend risking only 1-3%. Investors make the mistake of arbitrarily choosing a number, but you should be looking at percentages based on your specific account. When you only risk 1% of the capital in your trading account/exchange, you almost certainly assure your long-term survival in the game.

For example, if you have $10,000 to trade, any trade you make shouldn't allow you to lose more than $100-$300, or in other words 1-3%. That way, you can make multiple trades and while you will certainly lose a few, eventually you'll have winning trades that make up for your losses.

The way to make sure you're not risking more than 1-3% is simply to set stop-losses. From there, you can measure your risk-to-reward ratio. The risk-reward ratio measures the potential reward for every dollar you risk. Determining this will allow you to manage your risk and take more profitable trades.

Risk-to-Reward Ratio (RR)

You can determine whether or not to take a trade based on your RR ratio and then use smart position-sizing (1-3% of your portfolio). Three parameters are used to calculate RR: entry, stop loss and exit.

Here are 3 simple steps to do it:

1. Find out the distance of your stop loss
2. Find out the distance of your target profit
3. Calculate distance of target profit/distance of stop loss

An example: Let's assume your stop loss is $100 and profit target is $200. Apply the formula and you get... 200/100 = 2. This means you have a potential risk-reward ratio of 1:2.

>1:1 and Lower = Never trade
>1:1 = OK
>1:2 = Great
>1:3 and Higher = Ideal

PART 1. TRADING

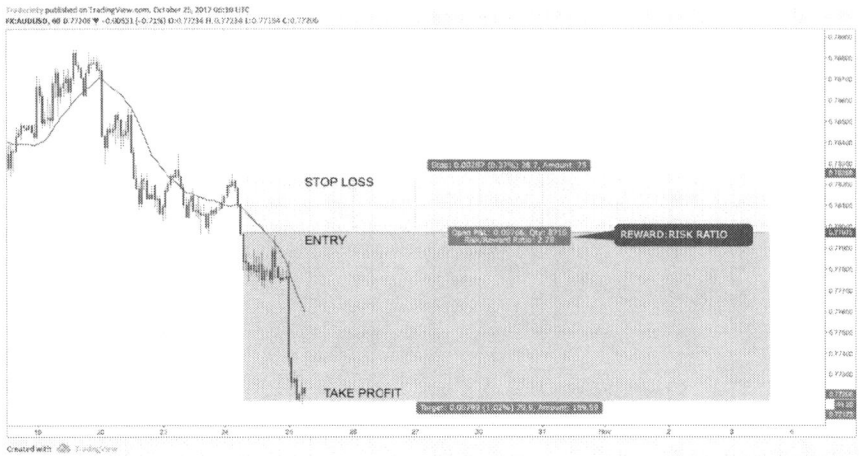

Once you know how much risk you're willing to take, you can work backwards to determine how much money you should put into a trade. So, let's assume you have $5000 in your trading account and don't want to risk more than 1% of your account. How much money should you risk in the trade?

The formula is: **((Size of your account * Risk % per trade) / (Entry Price—Stop Loss)) * Entry Price**.

Let's use the example below to determine how much $ you should put it in and plug in the formula.

    Pair: BTC/USD
    Entry Price: $9350
    Target Price: $10000
    Initial Stop Loss: $8650
    Your Account Size: $5000
    Risk Per Trade: 1%

CHAPTER 2. THE ONLY TRADING STRATEGY YOU WILL EVER NEED

=(($5000*0.01)/($9350-$8650))*$9350
=$668

Now, here's where a lot of traders get confused. Just because my account is $5000 doesn't mean that I couldn't make a trade using half of my capital ($2500) and still do really well over the long run. As long as a I set a stop loss that keeps my risk-to-reward ratio favorable (risking 1-3% of my capital), it's a good trade.

So, let's take another example. This time our stop loss is a bit tighter (target price and stop loss are closer)

Pair: BTC/USD
Entry Price: $9350
Target Price: $10000
Initial Stop Loss: $9193
Your Account Size: $5000
Risk Per Trade: 1%

Plugging in our formula to determine our position size, we get =(($5000*0.01)/($9350-$9193))*$9350=$2978. Yes, that means you can invest more than half of your trading account for a single trade! But it's ok, since your stop loss is set tightly and you're not actually risking much.

You don't have to make money on every trade to win. As long as you have more wins than you do losses, you can still come out on top. This is important to note because it gives you freedom—knowing that you will not, you cannot, win every single trade. And that's ok.

PART 1. TRADING

> *"Traders who understand this connection can quickly see that you neither need an extremely high win rate nor a large reward:risk ratio to make money as a trader."*
> —TRADECITY

HOW TO MAKE $779 IN 15 MINUTES WITH (ALMOST) ZERO TECHNICAL ANALYSIS

Let me show you how I made **$779 dollars in 15 minutes** without using (almost) any of the charting analysis I've described above. Traders have a tendency to overcomplicate things with fancy indicators, but those charts won't help you much when the price drops 90%. The point in showing this example is the importance of managing risk and buying when everyone else is selling.

As of writing this Bitcoin broke 6k and has been hovering around there for a while. It dropped to 4k. This is good. It means price movement, volatility, and cheaper Bitcoin (that could get cheaper yet!). It's not a market I am fond of trading as I prefer to trade big breakouts during bull markets. That said, currently many coins are correlated to Bitcoin, not all, but most—meaning when Bitcoin goes up, they go up. But oftentimes altcoins can have bigger price fluctuations relative to their price. So, I set out to find an altcoin that would meet two criteria. I want to see:

1. **Liquidity** (at least 2-3 million USD). You need trading volume, or else you won't be able to find buyers when you want to sell your coins.
2. **A big drop in price recently.** Big meaning 30% or more. Buy low, sell high. Most people do the opposite.

CHAPTER 2. THE ONLY TRADING STRATEGY YOU WILL EVER NEED

I was essentially looking for a dip buy. Taking a look, many coins fall into that category. I chose ETP (metaverse) because I liked how bloody the chart looked (a 75% drop in price in less than a week!) and it has relatively high volume. It looked like this:

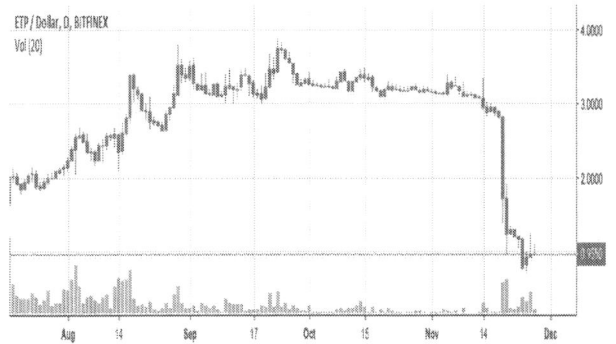

I didn't spend any time looking into the project, the fundamentals, the community, or pretty much anything else. I don't care about any of those things. I also don't know why the price dropped—whether that was because of a drop in BTC price or a news-related event. In fact, I've charted no lines on the graph. All I did was look at it and saw red (low price), volume, and the price hovering around prior support.

Next, I took $2,640 and entered a position when the price was at 88 cents, meaning I bought $2,640 worth of ETP at that price. My profit target was 20%, meaning that when the price hit roughly $1-$1.3, I would sell at that price. Why did I choose that target, and why isn't it a specific number? I looked at the point of resistance on the chart.

You might stop me here and say, *"Wait a second, I don't have that kind of money to just blow!"* Or *"I can't risk that much!"* There's a perception that you need to have a lot of money or take big risks or be a great technical analyst to make trades. Not really. You just have to be right some of the time, not even most of the time...just some of the time.

I didn't risk my $2,640—I only risked $150. In the scenario above, I set a stop loss at 83 cents. This means that if the price went to 83 cents, it would sell all my ETP token automatically. So the most I could lose would be $150. I set a price alert on Coinwink to alert me when the price went above $1. That way, I'd know when it was time to sell. This entire process of finding a coin, buying it, and setting an alert, took me all of about 15 minutes.

The price went up from .88 to 1.19 in one day. I sold all my ETP—one click, done. That $2640 turned into $3419, netting me $779.

A confession: I haven't traded in five months as the market has been choppy and bearish. Day trading is a losing strategy. When traders set financial goals or points at which to enter the market and trade, emotion takes over when it doesn't work out. Let the market tell you when it's ready—approach the market when there is volatility, and never risk a lot. It's as simple as setting a stop loss.

Never risk more than 1-5% of your money. Some people would say 1%. I could make 10 trades using this strategy and even if I was only right one or two of the times, I would still make money. I was risking $150 to make between $600-800.

Many professional or experienced traders might scoff at my example, noting my particular lack of technical analysis. I use this example not to show you the "best way" to trade, but the starting point of how *easy* it can be when you manage risk, even with minimal technical analysis.

CHAPTER 2. THE ONLY TRADING STRATEGY YOU WILL EVER NEED

In my interviews with traders, I asked them what their biggest challenges were. None of them said technical analysis or reading a chart. Their biggest challenges were largely mental and emotional.

Here are a list of the top three:

1. Properly taking profit and scaling out
2. Patience
3. Consistency and discipline

Once you're able to identify a good entry/exit point, all you need to do is manage risk and stick to your plan. You'll be a step ahead of most traders. Now let's talk about #2 and # 3, patience and discipline.

Chapter 3

DR. JEKYLL AND MR. HYDE

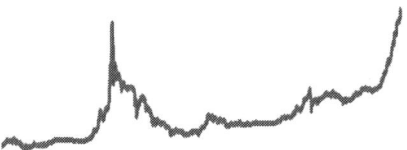

"With every day, and from both sides of my intelligence, the moral and the intellectual, I thus drew steadily nearer to the truth, by whose partial discovery I have been doomed to such a dreadful shipwreck: that man is not truly one, but truly two."
—ROBERT LOUIS STEVENSON, DR. JEKYLL AND MR. HYDE

Many natural insecurities, impulses, and tendencies manifest in a high stakes environment. They take control when we let envy, greed and anger drive our decision-making. We call these our animal instincts—this is our wild and irrational *Mr. Hyde*.

We also have another more analytical and rational side that allows us to deliberate by reason. This mode of thought gives us power to plan for the future, control our impulses, and even to think numerically. This is the good guy—our much-coveted *Dr. Jekyll*.

The bad news is that, as we discover in the famous 19th century novel, Dr. Jekyll and Mr. Hyde are the same person. We all have a bit of both personalities in us, and unless we make a conscious effort to reason with our Dr. Jekyll, we're prone to default into a Mr. Hyde.

The good news is that while we're all slaves to this duality of thinking/being, we *can* train ourselves to be more rational—even though it may not *feel* natural at first.

The first step is simply recognizing the strongest and most common tendencies that we identify with. Indeed, since Mr. Hyde is arguably a more default or natural state of being, we have to vigilantly observe our natural behavior when, in this case, trading cryptocurrencies.

All of the mistakes I have made trading crypto—perhaps in life—have come down to letting my emotions get the best of me. Here are some of the traps that I've personally fallen into:

- "If I don't have absolute control over the situation, then nothing will be ok." = Controlling behavior will result in constant over-checking of daily price swings.
- "Even a small loss equals a massive failure." = A strong aversion to loss will result in smaller trades.
- "It's either go big or go home." = A strong tendency for risky behavior results in big losses/total wipe-out.
- "I can skim over the details and things will work out." = Winging it leads to not planning your entry and exits on trades.
- Lots of fingernail biting = Even more fingernail biting.

How do we overcome some of these natural human tendencies and bad habits to develop our Dr. Jekyll?

STEP 1: SPEND TIME DEVELOPING MENTAL MODELS

Unless we have trained our minds to think in a certain way, we will automatically default to whatever habit-pattern is convenient or available. Psychologists call this the 'availability heuristic.'

Take time to understand the various mental models that exist (The Farnam Street Blog is great).[19] Each model is like a different pair of glasses—if you only have a blue pair of shades, your entire world will be tinted blue. When you try to have a conversation with someone wearing a red pair of glasses, there's going to be a fundamental lack of understanding between you.

The greater your collection of glasses, the greater variety of shades you will be able to interpret the world through, and the more angles from which you'll be able to tackle a problem.

The book by Mark Douglas, *Trading in the Zone*, helped me reframe my thinking in terms of probabilities (life is a lot like poker) when I was first starting out, and I have since revisited it several times.

While the book is a bit dated and deals mostly with stock trading, the concepts have more to do with *managing oneself* and thus equally apply to cryptocurrencies. The book helped me identify many of my own mental biases and is full of powerful lessons:

> *A probabilistic mind-set pertaining to trading consists of five fundamental truths: 1. Anything can happen. 2. You don't need to know what is going to happen next in order to make money. 3. There is a random distribution between wins and losses for any given set*

---

19 For more on mental models, see: https://fs.blog/mental-models/.

of variables that define an edge. 4. An edge is nothing more than an indication of a higher probability of one thing happening over another. 5. Every moment in the market is unique."
—MARK DOUGLAS

STEP 2: PATIENCE IS A VIRTUE

Give yourself ample time to reflect and strategize before making a trade. In anticipation of doing or having something pleasurable—like making a kickass trade—the neurochemical dopamine is released. When this happens, the areas of your brain that are responsible for complex planning and prediction (namely the prefrontal cortex, PFC) are hijacked.[20]

By making the choice to wait, you're giving your brain a chance to return to a baseline point where you're able to engage in complex and abstract thought processes. While hasty decisions lead to poor trades, waiting a bit longer gives our (more logical) Dr. Jekyll time to do his work.[21]

I always give myself at least a day before entering a trade—this gives me leeway to actually create a plan, rather than jumping in unprepared. While some might think a day is too long to wait, the number of times I regretted *making* a trade were much higher than the times

---

20 Daisy Dunne, "Are You Really in Control of Your Mind," *The Daily Mail*, http://www.dailymail.co.uk/sciencetech/article-4297698/Dopamine-brain-shape-decisions-make.html.
21 The more you exercise this thoughts process—of engaging your PFC to downregulate activity in the mesolimbic (i.e., dopamine-reward) pathway—the more likely you're to be able to do so in the future. The connections between neurons that are responsible for this process become strengthened through repetition. Essentially, this describes the neurological process of habit formation: you're rewiring your brain to practice healthy habits.

I regretted *not* making the trade. Besides, if a coin is breaking out it usually follows a 1-2-3-4 breakout pattern, so you can usually get in on the next dip anyways.

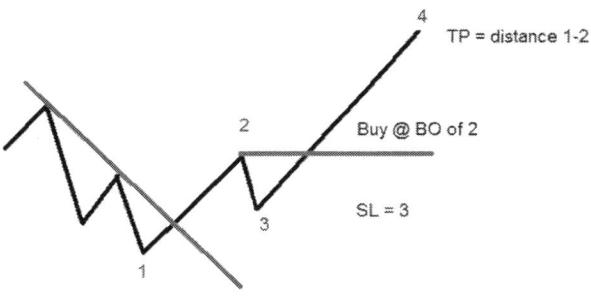

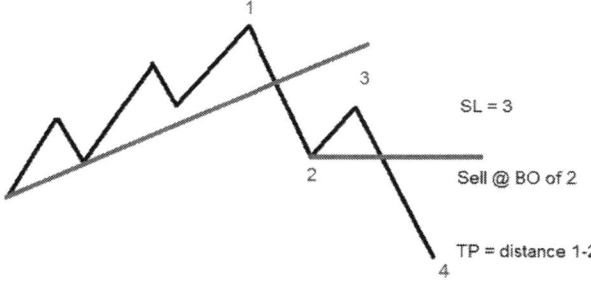

STEP 3: BODY, THEN MIND

Taking care of your body helps you make better decisions in life, so this is a given for trading as well.

Dialectical Behavior Therapy teaches the importance of doing incredibly simple things to avoid acting during a state of emotional over-arousal—this might involve deep breathing, taking a walk in nature,

PART 1. TRADING

engaging your senses (hot shower, ice on hand, smelling a flower) and so forth.[22]

After 30 minutes of sitting, 90% of your metabolism slows down. Simply standing up and walking for 5 minutes restarts it. It's so simple that it's *absolutely* dumb not to get off your butt every few minutes. Personally I meditate, exercise and have a daily sauna session that essentially washes away my stress enabling me to make better decisions. It doesn't matter what exercise you choose to do, just do *something*.

This is pretty basic stuff, I know, but it's easy to lose track of priorities when you're caught up in the grind and selling off your body heat to bitcoin miners *(foreshadowing of a Matrix apocalypse?)*[23]

In summary:

1. Spend time developing mental models.
2. Give yourself some breathing-room before making a trade (a day or more).
3. Take care of your body and your mind will be sharper, leading to less emotional trading.

> *The happiness of those who want to be popular depends on others; the happiness of those who seek pleasure fluctuates with moods outside their control; but the happiness of the wise grows out of their own free acts.*
> **—MARCUS AURELIUS**

---

22 "Dialectical Behavior Therapy," *Psychology Today*, https://www.psychologytoday.com/us/therapy-types/dialectical-behavior-therapy.
23 Jamie Redman, "Mining Cryptocurrencies With Human Body Heat," *Bitcoin.com*, https://news.bitcoin.com/these-dutch-researchers-are-mining-cryptocurrencies-with-body-heat/.

CHAPTER 3. DR. JEKYLL AND MR. HYDE

TRADING IS BORING

The best traders will tell you this: When you're doing it right and making consistent profits, trading is supposed to be boring. I wish I had known this before starting my trading journey.

> *"If investing is fun, if it's entertaining, you're probably not making any money."*
> —GEORGE SOROS

This may be counterintuitive. How could it ever be boring? There's oodles of money to be made and the markets are so volatile! So, why is trading and investing in crypto seemingly more exciting than the regular stock market?

Money. There's an aura of excitement that can quickly turn into exuberance when trading or investing in crypto. When emotions are high, logic is low and irrational thoughts quickly spiral out of control. People make impulsive buys and move into their parents' basements. The potential to pay off your student loans, mortgage, or take a debaucherous vacation to Cancun is certainly a good enough motivation. Because crypto is so new, too, it's still the Wild West so people feel like they have an advantage and can make money while it's still early days.

Ease of access: Going to a casino is less accessible—you have to physically go somewhere -whereas trading crypto is so easy you can do it with the swipe of a thumb wherever you are. If you thought Facebook was bad for people's mental health, crypto has the potential to be a lot more damaging, both psychologically (dopamine swipes to check your favorite coins) and financially (putting too much money on the line). Everybody and their grandmas are trading crypto.

PART 1. TRADING

What happens when you get too excited?

Trading on emotions is a sure way to get rekt.[24] Crypto brings out the worst in people, and many of the worst decisions I've made have been due to FOMO (fear of missing out). Emotions have a way of blinding us to the obvious.

When Ripple shot up to three dollars earlier many people were saying that it would shoot up to 10, 20 or 30 dollars. Nothing is impossible, but that would mean it would surpass the market cap of bitcoin—if one were to do any basic assessment you'd figure out that the chances of that happening are quite unlikely (at least in the short term, and at that particular point in time considering the market conditions).[25]

Social media and all of the talk around crypto doesn't make ignoring the hype any easier. Irrational behavior takes over when your favorite coin shoots up 200% and you reactively buy more, or McAfee shills a new project on Twitter that you buy immediately, or when you have a reaction (positive or negative) to CNBC or any article that comes out talking about "price action." The eccentric personalities in the crypto space don't make this any less emotional (Roger); they only feed fuel to the fire.

We listen to their hyperbole because it is what we want to hear. But we are equally good at conning ourselves. We take in the information that supports our trade, and ignore any information that is screaming:

---

24 Rekt is a slang version of "wrecked" that refers to losing a lot of your money.
25 Bitcoin dominates over 50% of the total market cap of all cryptocurrencies, and while it has fluctuated over time has remained at the top. Bitcoin's popularity tends to increase in bear markets where it's seen as a "safe haven" compared to more volatile altcoins. Keep in mind that the top 5-10 of cryptocurrencies ("large cap" coins) take longer to overtake each other and while they might be less risky, provide less of a potential reward when compared to mid or small cap coins that can make 10, 20 or 100x gains in much shorter time frames.

CHAPTER 3. DR. JEKYLL AND MR. HYDE

"This is a bad trade! Get out!" Psychologists call this mental trap the confirmation bias. Jim Paul, small town Kentucky trader turned governor of the Chicago Mercantile Exchange is one of many traders who have lost lots of money by following preexisting beliefs instead of a trading plan.

> *"Have you ever said to yourself, "No way! Is the market really down that far?" That's denial. Have you ever gotten mad at the market? Called it a name? Gotten angry at friends or family because of a position? That's anger. Ever begged the market or God to get you back to breakeven so you could get out? That's bargaining. Has a market loss ever changed your sleep or diet patterns? That's depression. Ever have a firm liquidate one of your positions? That's acceptance. Unless you have a plan, your potential loss is unknown and you can count on suffering through the Five Stages, losing more money as you go through each of the stages."*
> —JIM PAUL, WHAT I LEARNED LOSING A MILLION DOLLARS

When is it acceptable to be excited?

Of course, you might be excited about a project at first. That's a given. You spend time researching it, reading the white paper and understanding the value proposition. However, if you remain excited throughout your entire assessment of the project, you should ask yourself: Have you already made up your mind going in, or are you actually doing your due diligence?

In other words, being excited or passionate is fine to spark that initial fire (blockchain is a very exciting space, I know!), but we're better off using process, consistency and rational decision making to drive us forward, particularly when we're making financial decisions.

> *"Great passions are maladies without hope."*
> —GOETHE

How to make trading more boring

I'm borrowing this process from Jim Paul, who lost a million dollars trading; he knows a thing or two about psychological fallacies (and has since earned it back and written a book about the experience).

The decision-making process should be as follows:

1. Decide what type of participant you're going to be (trader/long-term investor)
2. Select a method of analysis (technical/fundamental)
3. Develop rules (when you will exit and enter)
4. Establish controls (stop losses)
5. Formulate a plan (write it down)
6. Stick to the plan (this is the hard part and the boring part)

If you've defined exactly when you're going to take profit off the table, then there's nothing emotional about the trade. The price goes up, you cash out your earnings, and you repeat. You check the charts once a day, or once a week for 10 minutes. It's boring.

When prices plummet, well, you've got a plan for that too. You've either got a stop-loss set or perhaps your trade is a long-term investment, in which case you don't care about cutting out. If you're holding on for the long term, you're not checking the price frequently. The investment is boring and not even on your mind. Obviously you should predefine your capital buckets (your allocation across different investment horizons and verticals); lack of clarity creates confusion and haste.

CHAPTER 3. DR. JEKYLL AND MR. HYDE

If you find yourself over thinking the price fluctuations (biting your nails as prices rise and fall), it usually means that you're taking too much risk. Solution: Reduce your risk exposure by setting stop losses or making smaller investments.

When trading becomes boring, you can enjoy life. You can detach yourself from your phone and computer screen and instead hang out with your friends, take a run in the park and spend time with your family.

TIME IS NOT MONEY

> *"I used to have a private jet, condo in Aspen and be the CEO of a Fortune 500 company ... then I switched to decaf."*
> —RADICAL ACCEPTANCE, TARA BRACH

When I started working full-time and found myself always wishing for more hours in the day, I came to embrace the business adage that *time = money*. So I calculated the average annual salary (50k) I was getting paid to work Monday–Friday, then divided it by the number of average annual working hours (roughly 2,087). My time was worth at least $24 per hour.

Monetizing each hour of my day caused me to see the world through a stress-filled lens that spiralled into counterproductive behavior. I would start thinking of my meetings with people in terms of money. This was problematic because, in my mind, I took the leap from time = money = people. People became money. Maybe this was a rookie mistake, but it's possible you've done it too.

Fortunately it didn't last long. I realized that money cannot be used to measure the quality of conversations, nor is it useful for assessing the relationships you might build, a valuable insight you might gain, or

PART 1. TRADING

the serendipitous friendships that emerge from meeting new people. Thinking that time is money also causes, not surprisingly, unhealthy habits like an excuse to work during your vacation or stay up too late to work (if you fall into this category, then perhaps it's time for a shift from the time = money mentality).

Money can be reinvested to produce more money, but time can't be spent to produce more time. Time is not money. *Time is time*, and *money is money*. Or, in other words, time = your existence. When we forget this, we can live our lives like "business" is life's top priority. More often than not, having squandered our precious time is a top deathbed regret. To lead a more meaningful life, I'd recommend the books *Power of Slow* and *Top 5 Regrets of Dying.*

PRICE-RELATED NEWS IS A WASTE OF TIME

The most pointless news articles are those that A) give a price prediction or market prediction, particularly in cryptocurrencies (bitcoin is going to a million!) or B) state their opinion on a person's affairs like it's the 'truth' (Elon is a fraud!).

> A = *fortune telling*
> B = *celebrity gossip*

Months ago ethereum founder, Vitalik Buterin, said that the cryptocurrency could go to zero; recently he was quoted saying that "we won't see 1,000 x growth anymore." [26] Perhaps he's being conservative,

---

26 David Meyer, "Ethereum Founder Vitalik Buterin Warns That Cryptocurrencies Could Drop to 'Near-Zero'," *Fortune*, http://fortune.com/2018/02/19/ethereum-price-ether-vitalik-buterin/.

CHAPTER 3. DR. JEKYLL AND MR. HYDE

knows something we don't, or is simply being realistic. But we've consistently been wrong about predicting things.

That's not to say that the price of a stock (or crypto) isn't *influenced* by media—of course it is, like when Tesla stock dropped after Elon Musk smoked a blunt on Joe Rogan's podcast. My favorite headline: "Tesla stock takes a hit—Elon Musk does the same." This is delicious clickbait. Like anything that John McAfee shills (although his shilling power has significantly decreased).

News and social media sentiment are a massive source of trading and investment fuel for hedge funds and high frequency traders. These events end up influencing price dramatically, but usually only temporarily as an equilibrium is found eventually (that said, you cannot compete with the speed of hedge funds and HFTs, so don't bother trying).

To the average person, though, not only does this not matter, it creates false confidence that we can accurately judge someone that we've never met on actions reported by skewed media agencies. We make a snap judgement to classify something as "good" or "bad" ("Elon is erratic!" or "He's just a misunderstood genius!"), but the world can rarely be fit into a neat bundle of good or bad.

The media creates a false dichotomy; it rarely reports events neutrally and tends to skew heavily towards eliciting a positive/negative emotion in the reader. The result being that we are led to respond in one of two simple, un-nuanced ways: we either like it, or we don't. Life, though, is *full* of nuance. In both examples above, rather than echoing the opinions of a Huffpost article, to really gain a deeper understanding of cryptocurrencies, we could study the asset's genesis and read everything on the topic...rather than trying to predict the

PART 1. TRADING

future. Instead of denouncing (or blindly praising) Elon, we could try and understand what he's doing and where he's coming from.

Undeniably, media reports can weigh heavily on market sentiment, but there are too many variables affecting price action that you cannot account for. We don't know what big whale is around the corner and going to dump tomorrow. We don't know what direction bitcoin regulations are going to go in.

The world is a very, very complicated place, with countless actors working behind the scenes and butterflies being stepped on (causing a series of uncertain chain reactions). Sometimes we forget this. This results in people forming automatic opinions based on articles designed to elicit exactly such an opinion, or arriving at their conclusion because somebody 'reputable' said so. The mistake would be to take any of these articles as objective — or, worse, use them as financial advice.

***Pro Tip:** When CNBC says buy, you sell. When CNBC says sell, you buy.

Chapter 4

10 LESSONS FROM AN EXPERT CRYPTO INVESTOR

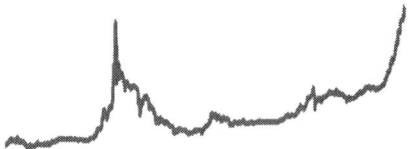

Chris Dunn is a mentor and investor that I've been following since the start of my crypto journey. I met him at a crypto meetup in Austin, Texas, which has the best baby-back ribs in the world. Chris has been trading for a long time having started off in commodities and futures, before moving into the crypto game early. He's the founder of a crypto education platform called Skill Incubator and a Venture Partner at NextGenVP.

He's one of the most patient investors I know and trades pretty infrequently—once every few months. Instead of day trading, he spends an inordinate amount of time researching investments and talking to founders of the projects he's interested in, well before he ever decides to pull the trigger. Chris adheres to the following trading rules.

PART 1. TRADING

1. DON'T DAY TRADE.

Once you get into day trading, it's hard to get out. I know. The market is always alive, and particularly in the world of crypto where trading doesn't stop on the weekend, it can feel like a 24/7 job. How can you reclaim your freedom?

It requires a shift in strategy from trading to investing. Don't put down what you can't afford to lose and start thinking about bigger gains. Why would you spend time picking up table scraps when you could get the whole chicken? The point: think longer term.

The majority of day traders lose money. That's a fact. It's also not good for your health; needless to say, staring at a computer screen all day as your blood pressure fluctuates at every red or green candle is not sustainable. Your friends and family are lonely. Go spend time with them.

2. INVEST LIKE AN ANGEL

A typical angel investor will invest in 10, 20 or even 30 companies at a time and put down 10k+ for each investment. The expectation is that most of the investments will fail, except hopefully one or maybe two. That one investment which produces 10-20x+ returns is expected to compensate for the losses of the other investments and make a healthy profit.

How do you select the companies? Most people will do a little research online on the fundamentals, price action, market cap, Telegram group, founders, tech, and growth opportunity. Take it a step further. Talk to people in the companies. Reach out to the founders or employees on LinkedIn. Ask them what their roadmap is, hiring plan, target

CHAPTER 4. 10 LESSONS FROM AN EXPERT CRYPTO INVESTOR

audience, plans for funding. Get the information from the horse's mouth, not the media. The more thorough your research, the more of a leg up you'll have.

You don't have to be in Silicon Valley to have access to valuable and actionable info. Information asymmetry can come from identifying early patterns or looking where other people aren't. For example, Tezos was involved in a big political/internal conflict, so many people pulled their money out and focused on other projects. But it was still the largest ICO in history, and as of the writing of this book, the price has remained fairly stable, projects are being built on top of it, and the tech is solid. Ask yourself: *What aren't people looking at? What do I know that most people don't know or are too distracted to see?*

In sum, in order to invest like an angel you should....

- Spend most of your time researching, and a fraction of it executing.
- Look for opportunities from information asymmetry.
- Assume you will lose all your money.

3. DON'T TRADE FOR INCOME

If you're trading to pay the bills, you're going to make bad decisions. When you need the money it's easy to become emotional, take bigger risks, and lose it all. This applies to most professions in which income is not predictable or consistent, like writing a book or creating a piece of art. You can make a lot of money, but you should keep your day job.

In trading and investing, it's a waiting game. Opportunities come along every now and then. The crypto-bull market in late 2017 was one such occasion, where practically any project you put money into would have gone up exponentially. Will that happen again? Maybe.

It makes sense to wait for that moment rather than try to squeeze out a little bit each day...you want to make sure you have ammo. Spend time building your skills, research low risk, high-reward opportunities, and be ready to pull the trigger when the time comes.

This advice applies to any business opportunity, though, not just trading. As I'm writing this a rumor is circulating that Amazon will be choosing a small city in Northern Virginia as their second US headquarters. It's not confirmed, but a commercial and business-savvy person would take advantage of this moment. Confirm the source and then start planting the seeds for a business—there will be thousands of people moving to that city to work at Amazon, which means many people will be looking for information on that city—from relocation and travel to where to buy stuff. You could write a travel guide for that area or create a product for that specific demographic. Strike while the iron is hot.

4. "IT ONLY TAKES ONE TRADE."

There's some truth to the 'get rich quick' saying. On one hand, instant riches is not really feasible and depends on your definition of "quick." On the other hand, it's less about luck than people think, and it would be a lot more within reach if we were all a bit more patient. Would you wait three years to make half a million dollars? I know I would. But most people don't have the patience or the discipline. Part of this stems from our society's emphasis on action, which is exacerbated by the average job in which we are paid for our time rather than our results. It's very hard to detach this feeling of having to "do something" from actual progress—often times we're pretending to be busy and not making any actual progress. It can be simply a matter of doing our research, creating our plan, and *waiting* for the right moment.

I know a guy who spent weeks and weeks researching crypto projects and became convinced of the potential of the technology of a certain project, so he invested $10k USD. He was right. A few months later, the token was listed on a major exchange and soared 100x in price. It was a liquid coin, a big project. He quite literally made a million dollars and cashed out. Of course, he could have invested in a bunch of smaller projects, or day traded along the way (which he did very minimally) like most people, but that would not have set him up for big success. When you find yourself becoming impatient trading, just remind yourself: it only takes one trade (to make a lot of money).

5. YOU CAN LOSE 50% OF YOUR TRADES AND STILL BE PROFITABLE IF YOU MANAGE RISK PROPERLY.

This may seem counterintuitive, so let me illustrate with four trades made over a period of 3 months:

Trade 1:
- You buy $5,000 worth of X coin and set a stop loss at $4,900
- Result: You get "stopped out" (your stop loss triggers) and lose -$100

Trade 2:
- You buy $5,000 worth of X coin and set a stop loss at $4,900
- Result: You get "stopped out" (your stop loss triggers) and lose -$100

Trade 3:
- You buy $5,000 worth of X coin and set a stop loss at $4,900
- Result: You get "stopped out" (your stop loss triggers) and lose -$100

You're getting sad at this point. You keep making shitty trades and losing money. But you've only lost $300.

PART 1. TRADING

It's ok, hang in there.

And then... on Trade 4:

- You buy $5,000 and set a stop loss at $4,900
- Result: You wait patiently for 3 weeks and the price increases by 30% to $6,500 — not uncommon in the crypto world. Your profit is $1500 — $300 (on your previous 3 losses) = $1200.

Of course, along the way we're prone to all sorts of psychological biases and fallacies. If our second or third trade don't make money, we might start to question our decision-making ability and skill. Certainly that's worth assessing. But as long as we have stop losses, mental or automatic, or some way to make sure we don't lose all of our money, then we can emerge profitable in the end.

6. "YOU WILL MAKE EVERY MISTAKE IN THE BOOK. DON'T BEAT YOURSELF UP WHEN YOU MAKE MISTAKES, JUST LEARN AND TRY NOT TO MAKE THE SAME MISTAKE TWICE."

This lesson is so painfully true. Even after watching countless Youtube videos, planning trades, and reading books on investing and trading psychology, I still screwed everything up. I got scammed, twice. I sold too early, I pulled my trades out because of fear, I didn't sell when I should have and lost money. I regretted trades. And then I made the same mistakes again.

Things are always different on the battlefield. The biggest mistake I made was not training my mind. I was like the impatient kid that reached for the cookie or marshmallow too soon. It sounds really basic, but I had to take care of the rest of my life before I could make any good decisions trading. That means getting enough sleep, eating well, and exercising. It's basic, I know, but trust me it's a lot easier to make a good decision when your eyes aren't bloodshot and you're not constipated and worrying about rent.

Accept you will fail at times. But keep getting better. It won't happen overnight. And remember that even if you lose a few times, you can always bounce back—*it only takes one trade.*

7. "THE 3 BIGGEST PROBLEMS FOR TRADERS ARE OVER-TRADING, HESITATING ON ENTRIES, AND CLOSING POSITIONS PRIOR TO PROFIT TARGETS WHEN THE TRADE IS STILL INTACT."

As you observe your own trading behavior, keep an eye out for these big mistakes:

Over trading: You try to catch every single move. You look at every indicator and every small movement in price as an indicator that you should buy or sell. The solution here is to create a plan and write it down on a piece of paper, and identify your capital—as we discussed previously. Stick to the plan.

Hesitating on entries: This usually implies you're not confident in your plan for some reason. Maybe you need to do more research. Or, you could be scared because you're taking too much risk. Put less on the table. And remember, you can lose on trades...as long as you win the big ones.

Closing position prior to profit targets: This may not seem like a big deal, but you can leave a lot on the table here. The other side of greed is being too stingy. In particular new markets in crypto tend to blow away profit targets, so it's usually a good idea to take profit *along the way up,* setting multiple profit targets. And even leave a little bit of a runner if you think the price action is very bullish.

8. TRADING ISN'T ABOUT PICKING EXACT TOPS AND BOTTOMS IN A MARKET—IT'S ABOUT CATCHING THE MEAT OF A MOVE.

There are a lot of people who suffer from analysis paralysis. They make the perfect charts and wait for the perfect move—but there is no perfect move and it never comes, so they lose money. The charts will never align perfectly (it's very rare). Look at multiple indicators and even if you're a little bit late on a breakout, you can still do really well, as long as you enter the darn trade! Don't think "I *shoulda coulda woulda,*" and not take a trade because you're a tiny bit late. Regret is bound to make you more timid and god-forbid do something stupid like revenge-trade (trading as a reaction to a loss).

9. DON'T TURN A SMALL LOSING TRADE INTO A MASSIVE LOSING INVESTMENT.

New investors don't get how hedge fund managers can see minus hundreds of millions on their accounts and not kill themselves (some do). Size is relative. It's going to hurt a bit no matter what. No one likes losing money. But trading, or any investment, can be surprisingly unemotional. You can make it less emotional by hedging risk (stop losses), and if you're bleeding money then pull out early and stomach your losses.

10. TURN YOUR FOMO INTO JOMO.

There are so many things that you could have done. Your fear of missing out, though, will lead you to make impulsive decisions. Instead, focus on practicing your one kick 10,000 times, and ignore whatever else is around you. You WILL miss trades—we all do. You can't possibly take all the opportunities and by choosing one you're forgoing another. That is okay.

Define where you're focusing your time and effort. Once that is defined, you can turn your Fear of Missing Out (FOMO) into Joy of Missing Out (JOMO). You can be confident and happy that you took the trade or investment you did. While others are wallowing in regret, you're smiling in confidence.

Chapter 5

FIVE THINGS BRUCE LEE TAUGHT ME ABOUT TRADING

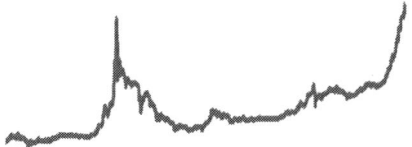

#1 "I FEAR NOT THE MAN WHO HAS PRACTICED 10,000 KICKS ONCE, BUT I FEAR THE MAN WHO HAS PRACTICED ONE KICK 10,000 TIMES."

The wise trader has a wide ranging toolkit to choose from. Whether you buy or build trading tools, your trading system will provide all the essentials, but don't mistake the abundance of tools to mean that you should use all of them. Experiment at first, yes, but one cannot possibly master all of them, nor should one try.

By becoming proficient at *one or two* strategies, you can gain an edge. Your deadly flying side kick to the throat will destroy your opponent. You want to master the trading tactics that allow you to consistently defeat the markets—not with a scattered approach or a range of semi-powerful moves, but with a K.O.

PART 1. TRADING

The best traders and investors will find their edge and hone their skills daily. They will read everything they can about their method of choice, watch all the Youtube videos, listen to all the podcasts and talk to others who are more skilled than themselves.

You can become the expert in hunting for degenerate micro-cap coins on Cryptopia and focus on making 100x gains once a year. You may be adept at knife-catching big, bloody dips where other traders are too fearful to go. Or you may get really good at setting smart stop losses and train your mind to buy low and sell high. Perhaps you become the technical expert at setting up profitable mining rigs, or staking, or whatever. Maybe you ignore trading all together and sell shovels to the gold miners, establishing a niche and a profitable bitcoin-related merchandise and e-commerce business.

The possibilities are endless, but the point is to find your deadly kick and practice it over and over.

#2 "IN THE MIDDLE OF CHAOS LIES OPPORTUNITY."

Big Black Swan events like the Great Depression or the housing bubble in 2008 provided ample opportunity for smart investors to swoop in and buy when everybody else was selling. These are obvious examples of how when market sentiment is low, chaos reigns, and people make emotional decisions. Fear is at its highest during these periods since people don't know how low prices will go. Extreme events provide the greatest opportunity for anybody willing to take the risk.

The scale of the event doesn't have to be huge in order for you to take advantage of the situation. Fortunately, in newer markets and industries plenty of chaos exists. It's a matter of taking time to observe before taking action and formulating a decent plan. That's more than

CHAPTER 5. FIVE THINGS BRUCE LEE TAUGHT ME ABOUT TRADING

most people do. For example, when ETH or BTC or any other coin announce a fork, usually people flock to buy the coin to get their free money. The same with airdrops. Then, when the media picks up the ICO, everyone gets into a frenzy over buying up the coin only to get wrecked on the coin's subsequent way down a couple of days later.

Savvy traders keep track of the dates for these events and buy before the media picks up the news. They set a target, keep an eye on the market, and sell for good returns, instead of hodling and hoping for the best. They've structured what could've been a potentially emotional and chaotic situation into an unemotional buy and sell. They didn't lose any sleep over it.

Often times, the conditions for chaos can be identified. When a crypto exchange is acquired, panic could ensue. What if investors' coins are locked in or delisted (it happens) because of the acquisition? Before this happens, it's probably best to diversify or take money you're not willing to lose off that exchange. The art of making money is also the art of not losing money. Every event reported in the news, company acquisition, new blockchain project, government regulation, partnership announcement, listing of a coin, delisting of a coin, legal dispute, technical failure, endorsement, airdrop, fork, and pretty much anything you can think of has the potential to be disruptive to price. Be vigilant and monitor price movers and, whenever possible, manage related price risk.

PART 1. TRADING

#3 "EMPTY YOUR MIND, BE FORMLESS. SHAPELESS, LIKE WATER. IF YOU PUT WATER INTO A CUP, IT BECOMES THE CUP. YOU PUT WATER INTO A BOTTLE AND IT BECOMES THE BOTTLE. YOU PUT IT IN A TEAPOT IT BECOMES THE TEAPOT. NOW, WATER CAN FLOW OR IT CAN CRASH. BE WATER MY FRIEND."

We shouldn't force our desires onto the market. Rather, we should stay shapeless and be ready to go where the market takes us. If you look at macro trends and see that we're in a bear market, don't trade as if you're in a bull market because of "hope"—this is not a strategy. Accept what the market is, taking into account that the big wave today could come crashing down tomorrow.

When we set profit targets based on our desires, we are basically pushing our desires onto the market. It doesn't make sense to choose an arbitrary number like $1 million dollars and say that we'd like to make that much within one year. While it's a nice round number, it's impossible for you to predict how much you will make.

You're not trading precious metals like gold, which barely move in price over a five-year period. you're trading highly volatile cryptocurrencies that can disappear overnight. The good news is that you could make much more than $1 million, while the bad news is you could only make half that much. Don't put your mind inside one box.

Those who have a basic knowledge/interest in crypto tend to make their interest a prominent aspect of their identity. Observe the Twitter chatter: "So and so is the Bitcoin guy; while so and so is Ripple; and so and so likes Ethereum."

CHAPTER 5. FIVE THINGS BRUCE LEE TAUGHT ME ABOUT TRADING

So, crypto, for many, is more than just an interest/activity—it's who they are, rather than what they do. These digital coins really seem to consume many. This leads these 'analysts' to assuming an inflexible position whereby they're not able to analyze the market rationally and make decisions which counter beliefs previously held with conviction. Be fluid and open to disconfirming information.

#4 "ABSORB WHAT IS USEFUL, DISCARD WHAT IS USELESS AND ADD WHAT IS SPECIFICALLY YOUR OWN."

Watching crypto news analysts conducting "price analysis" on a specific currency is a waste of your time. The media has a quota of articles to write daily, and the easiest type of article to write is one in which they attempt to predict the future, but essentially say nothing. You can safely ignore these articles. You're better off learning the skills required to make your own decisions without the media. However, there are some cases in which you should pay attention to the news— for example, to assess market sentiment. When a crypto project is getting a lot of negative media, is there truth to the matter, or more likely is the media doing what it does (writing clickbait articles) and the coin is actually ripe for an increase in price? Not a rule of thumb necessarily, but what we see in the media can be a good sign that we should do the opposite.

Instead of looking to analysts, you will do better developing your own competencies. When I entered the recruitment market, among tech giants, many people told me it was a spinning revolving door. For four years I helped tech companies like Google, Amazon and Facebook find and retain top talent by developing my own network. This required me to meet with thousands of people, review countless resumes, and consult with job seekers on their careers. I worked very closely with the tech companies, befriended their hiring managers,

PART 1. TRADING

and picked their brains on everything from product and monetization to sales strategy. While I'm less qualified to assess the technical specs of a product on Github, I am confident that I have a decent level of insight into the dynamics of hiring talent, which undoubtedly contributed to the success of these companies.

A friend of mine is very good at managing several trading bots. He even builds his own. He's gotten to the point where it's profitable for him, even though he's been scammed and lost money, and he knows more about trading bots than most people. When someone tells him "you can't make money from trading bots" or "it's too risky," it goes in one ear and out the other. He has proven that it's not true, at least not in his case. Everyone should invest time into diving deep into at least one area, building off of existing skills, and finding that unique intersection of personal interest and opportunity. It's a lot easier if you actually enjoy it!

#5 "THE SUCCESSFUL WARRIOR IS THE AVERAGE MAN, WITH LASER-LIKE FOCUS."

You don't need to have three computer screens, lots of trading capital or be a guru in technical analysis to make money. The art of practicing the daily kick (improving diligently on one technique rather than spreading yourself thin), building rockets, or sweeping the floor only requires a small amount of action daily. It's about getting 1% better. The key is doing it deliberately. We falsely overestimate what we need to get started. It's little steps.

Warren Buffett, amongst other famous investors, reads each day for hours and hours on end. He's not just reading for fun. He knows that information asymmetry will give him a leg up in the game and so he spends every day learning just a little bit more. New media and

CHAPTER 5. FIVE THINGS BRUCE LEE TAUGHT ME ABOUT TRADING

analyst sites crop up daily in the blockchain and cryptocurrency markets contributing to the information overload. Keeping current would overwhelm anyone, which is another reason why I wouldn't suggest selecting 20 strategies and trying to become good at them. You'll be mediocre at best and never get an edge.

The actions that require you to gain any sort of knowledge asymmetry are pretty basic. Consume information about a particular topic and learn as much about it as you can. The newer the topic the better, as it's less likely many people have had time to truly master it. For example, if you decide that Security Tokens and STOs are the future, you could take a few small actions that will compound over time. Start building a list of companies that are in the STO space, follow their activity and join their mailing lists. Reach out and speak directly to their founders, go to their events where you can be 'in the know' and ahead of the curve and engage in real conversations. While others are trading their money away, you're building up a knowledge base and an edge.

These small actions could also include... interviewing 10 people in STO companies for your blog (or whatever), going to a blockchain event, reading one article about STOs every day, finding the experts in the industry and establishing a relationship with them/taking them out for coffee/having a Skype call, and sharing what you've learned with others. Do this every day and every week and you will have developed an edge.

Chapter 6

CREATE SYSTEMS, NOT GOALS

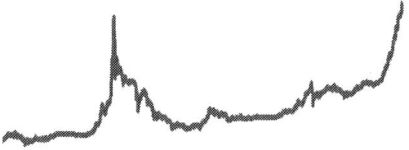

The two founders of WhatsApp applied for a job at Facebook back in 2009, but their applications were rejected. So they went on to start a company that they eventually sold to Facebook for $22 billion.

Jan and Brian did not start WhatsApp with the plan of selling to Facebook, of course. They simply hammered down on an idea they believed in, used their skills, and probably benefited from a bit of luck. They "exited" successfully—not that exiting was ever the goal.

But imagine if they *had* started the company with the goal of being bought out within a specific time for a specific amount of money. It's likely that they would have put the wrong incentives in place; they may have tried to monetize too quickly or sacrificed product quality. In the end, they probably would have also low-balled themselves.

Then is focusing on money always counterproductive to achieving big dreams? We still need to set goals, but how do we even start to create

PART 1. TRADING

goals when we're venturing into unknown territory? Why do so many of us never get started on pursuing our big dreams?

DON'T SET GOALS, SET SYSTEMS

Shedding a few pounds or running a marathon have proven formulas for success—follow them to the tee and you're likely to come out victorious. However, the greater number of variables there are that could affect the outcome, the more difficult it becomes to predict what will work and what won't.

A concept I've picked up from crypto: *Traders who set financial goals almost always lose.* Why? Because you can't control the market. People try and force their will on the market to no avail (I want the market to go up in price so it benefits *ME*), resulting in emotional decision-making, like panic-selling when the market plummets.

It's the person who screams "Buy bitcoin, it's going to the moon!" when the price is at an all time high of $20k, who loses his life savings a couple of months later. The market doesn't care what he thinks. It's like going to the poker table saying "I will make X amount of money today!" It just doesn't make sense because we don't have that kind of control over the universe.[27]

Instead of trying to make the market fit your financial goals, the wiser choice is to create systems that allow you to make higher-probability winning trades. In the case of trading, that might mean always setting

---

27 Many people trade because they crave control (perhaps even bordering on OCD sometimes); and this leads to disillusionment. I think this is part of the appeal of trading to many—and *The Wolf of Wall Street* demonstrated how this idea (of an omniscient trader who can control and predict with absolute precision) appeals to many. I'm proposing a healthier, more well-balanced approach.

CHAPTER 6. CREATE SYSTEMS, NOT GOALS

a stop loss, whereby if the price goes below a certain point, you always agree to sell. That way you avoid being completely annihilated and losing all your money.

The other system could be to wait 24 hours before executing a trade, that way you avoid emotional decision making. Similar to replying to a heated email, this tactic will allow you to think things through and remain cool-headed. Success comes down to setting up systems.

In her book about decision making, *Thinking in Bets*, Annie Duke makes the point that our life is more like poker and less like chess, as we don't have all of the pieces in front of us.

She goes on to explain:

> *Poker, in contrast, is a game of incomplete information. It is a game of decision-making under conditions of uncertainty over time (Not coincidentally, that is close to the definition of game theory.). Valuable information remains hidden. There is also an element of luck in any outcome. You could make the best possible decision at every point and still lose the hand, because you don't know what new cards will be dealt and revealed. Once the game is finished and you try to learn from the results, separating the quality of your decisions from the influence of luck is difficult.*

There are simply too many factors to consider to sit down and confidently say, "Yes, my goal is to become a multi-millionaire by this age." When it comes to starting a business, often, focusing on money is the antithesis to innovation; you earn proportionally to the amount of value you're adding.

PART 1. TRADING

If you think focusing on money in trading or investing in crypto is inevitable, you could benefit from a lesson in human motivation. Behavioral economists tell us that chasing after money is unlikely to be a true motivator, at least over the long run. Remember the saying is not "money is the root of all evil," but "the **LOVE** of money is the root of all evil."

One solution is to focus on your mental, physical and emotional health. Setup systems that don't require you to check your phone every 10 minutes or cause you to worry. Trust that the road will lead you to financial gain.

The point: Life is like poker, not chess. When there are several variables involved, we can never have 100% certainty. To improve our odds, we should create systems that serve us in the long run.

We see now that the goal-setting approach can fall flat on its face, particularly when defining monetary goals. To set a time-specific AND number-specific goal for personal wealth goes both ways: It is potentially limiting; indeed, maybe you can make oodles more money than you think! Or, it sets you up for disappointment; maybe you give up and stop short of a big win because the goal is too out of reach, hence demotivating.

Here are five systems that pushed me in the right direction. These are not all crypto-specific, anyone can use them, but they are systems I've built to keep a healthy, positive attitude and sane when the markets were in the gutter. Note that I continue to do these activities, and at this point they've turned into habits.

Read a lot. From Warren Buffet to Jeff Bezos, leaders are all habitual readers. If you set a goal to read 50 pages every day for 3 months, this could result in goal fatigue, and you will likely 'check-out' without processing the content. You want to focus on quality rather than quantity. Instead, create a reading system: read something every day—no matter how short or long. Sometimes you'll read less than 50 pages, other days a lot more. You'll average out around the same overall total, without the added pressure, and thus likely increase your actual focus and retention of the material.

The daily journal. The simple act of getting thoughts on paper can produce less stress, better goal-planning, a higher mode of self-reflection and overall greater happiness. Writing in cursive handwriting also helps conceptual development and memory, so the benefits extend far beyond just putting thoughts on paper.

Morning routines. Having a defined, solid morning routine is one of the most important habits one can build. It's the proverbial 'keystone habit,'[28] or the habit (more precisely, a series of habits) that can lead to other good habits. If marijuana is a gateway to more drugs, then a morning routine is a gateway to more success; planted firmly on the opposite side of the spectrum, although perhaps no less addictive.

Evenings routines. If you can get good sleep, then you'll likely feel refreshed in the morning even if your morning routine is drinking a cup of coffee and reading a few pages of a book. I keep it simple. I turn down the thermostat to a cool temperature, turn my phone onto airplane mode, and eat an egg before I go to bed.

---

28 Keystone habits lead to the development of multiple good habits. They start a chain effect in your life that produces a number of positive outcomes. Exercise doesn't just lead to more energy, but also to healthier eating, better concentration, and a desire to set higher goals.

PART 1. TRADING

Listen to podcasts every day. A wealth of amazing content is created every day. Tuning into podcasts will give you new ideas and teach you new things that you can apply in business and life. I use the Overcast.fm app and listen to all episodes on 2x speed. Some of my favorite podcasts are *Off the Chain, The Flippening, Unchained, Block Zero, The a16z Podcast, The Tim Ferriss Podcast, and Joe Rogan.* *I've provided a full list of my favorite podcasts and crypto resources at the end of the book.*

Chapter 7

YOUR RISK MANAGEMENT PLAN

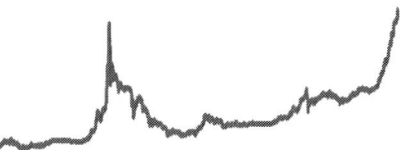

If we fail to anticipate the unforeseen or expect the unexpected in a universe of infinite possibilities, we may find ourselves at the mercy of anyone or anything that cannot be programmed, categorized, or easily referenced.
—AGENT FOX MULDER, THE X-FILES

There are a dozen or more ways that you can get scammed. This includes email phishing scams, telegram scams, fake ICO's, and the more recent SIM swapping scams. You don't need to be a security expert to see that as we build our technology on more and more layers, the more susceptible we are to a security breach. If your phone number is the main fail safe recovery for your crypto exchange, and all of your money is on crypto exchanges, then this leaves you open to attack.

Diversification doesn't only apply as an *investment* strategy (buying 10 different altcoins), but as a *protection* strategy that we can implement

PART 1. TRADING

to effectively hedge our bets when storing and transferring crypto. In other words, store your assets across a range of platforms and mediums, both online and offline. Diversification is the main solution to counterparty risk. It's really simple in theory, but it can take a bit of effort in practice.

Through my own mistakes I've found that the biggest risks are due to human error. This includes not setting proper stop losses or making emotional trading decisions without back up plans. That is where the greatest risk lies. A little bit of preparation can go a long way.

COUNTERPARTY RISK

Counterparty risk = the risk that the other party (the counterparty) of a financial contract will not live up to its contractual obligations

Keeping large chunks of money on exchanges is a bad idea. Historically, exchanges have done a very poor job in protecting consumer funds (Mt Gox, Bitfinex, Coincheck...). Coinbase is FDIC insured, so that's a plus, but you're still putting your trust in another person's hands. That said, keeping some on exchanges, especially if you're an active or semi-active trader, is useful and of course necessary.

Keep trading capital on exchanges but never use it as a "checkings" or "savings" account. If you haven't done so, I recommend setting up accounts on at least three or four exchanges. I have at least five different exchanges I personally use. While you can't eliminate 100% of the risk, you can spread it out. For your 'long term capital bucket,' you should keep those funds in an offline wallet where there is no risk of an exchange getting hacked.

CHAPTER 7. YOUR RISK MANAGEMENT PLAN

LIQUIDITY

Liquidity = the availability of liquid assets to a market or company

When there is low trading volume on an exchange and not enough buyers, it can be difficult to sell your coins. This can put you in a very sticky situation. If the price of a coin plummets and you can't sell it, all you can do is painfully take your losses. "Pump and dump" groups (Palm Beach being the most notorious) coordinate the buying and selling of a coin in order to artificially inflate the price, taking advantage of low liquidity and selling very quickly, leaving everyone else to pick up the scraps.

There will always be a risk of low liquidity when you're trading *low* market cap coins. It's largely unavoidable, so the best you can do in that case is invest small amounts that you're willing to lose. The reason you would invest in a small cap coin in the first place is because you have some expectation that its value could increase 10x or 100x (not unheard of in the wild world of crypto!).

Otherwise, if you want to avoid liquidity issues, stick to mid cap and large cap coins. Second, find exchanges that have high liquidity— Coinbase, Binance, Bittrex and so forth. When you have large cap coins on a small exchange you can still run into liquidity issues. I've never had a problem trading bitcoin or ethereum on Bitfinex or Bittrex.

At some point, though, if you have a lot of money in crypto, say six, seven, or more digits, this could become an issue if you want to sell. In these cases, you can find an "over the counter" crypto broker that can connect you to buyers and sellers with big pockets (a quick Google or Linkedin search will bring up several).

BEWARE OF SCAMS

One study found that 80% of ICOs either haven't delivered on a product or were flat-out scams.[29]

Caught up in the exuberance of making big gains I've fallen prey to scams myself—twice as if I didn't learn my lesson the first time. I remember on one occasion a pre-sale for the Quantstamp ICO claimed to be closing in 24 hours. I did a poor job of the due diligence and rushed to buy, sending over one ether (around $400 at the time), convinced that time was running out.

Scammers are smart. They had replicated the real website almost exactly, but had simply changed the URL to quants*lamp*, with an L. Considering my impatience and lack of attention to detail, I fell for it. I've spoken to many crypto traders who have gotten scammed for much more. Some have been pretty much wiped out. Many gave up, but others took their loss to heart, learned from their mistakes and started small again, often succeeding in rebuilding their portfolios. There will always be bad actors trying to take something from you — your time, money, well-being. Manage your risk wisely but don't give up after a couple of negative experiences.

Two ways to avoid scams:

1. *Don't rush into anything.* When you see anything that is 'time sensitive' you should automatically be skeptical. Double check the website, spend 1-2 days researching the project. Don't give money to strangers on online forums. Nowadays all crypto projects go

---

[29] C. Edward Kelso, "Study Claims 80% of ICOs are Scams," *Bitcoin.com*, https://news.bitcoin.com/80-of-icos-are-scams-only-8-reach-an-exchange/.

CHAPTER 7. YOUR RISK MANAGEMENT PLAN

through a KYC (know your customer) process that requires your ID, and often takes a couple of days for verification. If you don't have to go through this process it should be a red flag.

2. *Always split money being invested into smaller amounts.* Regardless of whether you're investing in an ICO, setting up a trade or moving money between exchanges, every transaction you make should be done with small amounts to start with. If it's a scam or you accidentally mess up the address you're sending money to, your money is gone. There are no banks here. Nobody is going to recover your key or money for you if you send it to the wrong address. It's much easier to stomach losing $100 then $1000.

NOT SETTING STOP LOSSES

I know I've said this already, but it bears repeating. You can make money. You can do well. Often it takes time. But the name of the game is to not get impatient, make big gambles and get wiped out. Then it's game over.

Remember what Chris Dunn said—"It only takes one trade." He means that it only takes one trade per year to make lots of money. If you do your due diligence and research, and play your cards right you will be far ahead of most people who trade daily and lose money. It's also a lot less stressful. There's no need to sit in front of your computer every day checking prices.

None of that matters if you get wiped out, though. I repeat myself a lot here, but it's critical. The easiest way to avoid getting wiped out is to set a stop loss. When the price goes below X, you've automatically triggered the sell. That's it. You'll never lose all your money that way. Of course, diversify across exchanges and follow the other tips outlined here.

One objection people have to setting stop losses is that you can't account for "fake outs." In a typical scenario, the price drops—usually set up by some whales—enough to trigger lots of stop losses, and then shoots back up. This can be very frustrating. You can do two things here.

1. *Mental stop losses.* You can set a "mental stop loss" and watch the markets like a hawk—set price alerts. That way you give yourself a little flex room for the range of a stop loss (if you set it at $1 and it drops to 98 cents, then shoots back up, it'd be a shame for your stop loss to trigger). This would apply to a short-term trade (I don't recommend this technique unless you're already a relatively experienced trader).
2. *Increase your stop loss range.* When a coin breaks support levels, it usually signals a downward trend, and the coin could drop a lot lower. But that doesn't mean there is an "exact" support number. You can take on a bit more risk and set a wider range for your stop loss. Identify the previous point in the market where support would break, and set your stop loss a little bit lower than that, rather than setting it exactly at the level of support (for example, if support levels are $100, set your stop loss at around $95).

SCARED? YOU'RE TAKING TOO MUCH RISK

Presented with an opportunity to buy a speculative financial product, the fear-radar goes off. Or maybe it's the bullshit radar. The dial is spinning out of control and tons of questions are swimming in your mind. *How do I know this isn't fake? What if it's a scam? What if I lose all my money? Which coin should I choose? How do I store this? Is this legal? Who can I trust?*

These are all good questions that should be addressed, but they're probably the wrong questions to ask at first. There's a simple reason

CHAPTER 7. YOUR RISK MANAGEMENT PLAN

that these questions pop up. You should write this down and refer back to it when you feel nervous or when you find yourself too concerned about an investment. And that reason is simply, *if you're scared, you're taking too much risk.* It doesn't make sense to take a big chunk of your money, your savings, or god forbid, borrow money or mortgage your house, to invest. That's too much risk.

THE CEILING IS TOO HIGH

Research on the behavior of gamblers found that creating a casino with high ceilings and a more pleasant atmosphere had a psychologically "restorative" effect on the gamblers. Specifically, they felt more positive emotions and less stress; as a result they took **bigger risks, spent more and lost far more.**[30]

You could interpret that literally and avoid making decisions when you're feeling overly positive or when you're too comfortable. And taken very literally you should probably avoid making your trades in rooms with high ceilings! Not a bad idea.

But I think a metaphorical parallel could be drawn to the "high ceiling" that bitcoin offers — so much more than just financial rewards are on offer. Cryptocurrencies offer the potential to restructure the most basic assumptions/foundations upon which our society is based, and that's exciting.

The sky may be the limit, but irrational exuberance and hope can lead to risky decisions that leave your bank account empty. There's

---

30 Ceilings and Gambling:
See http://journals.sagepub.com/doi/abs/10.1177/0013916509341791, or see https://www.wired.com/2012/03/the-psychology-of-casinos/.

PART 1. TRADING

certainly a middle path—appreciate the potential of the industry by playing an active role in the community, but be realistic about the downside. Take profit in USD and cash out when you've made some money.

TAX STRATEGY

Whether or not you are making money, crypto gains and losses will likely affect your taxes. You are paying taxes on your crypto gains, aren't you? Or are you part of the 50 percent of investors with unreported US cryptocurrency tax liabilities? The unpaid portion of total crypto tax liabilities of $25 billion, estimates Fundstrat Global Advisors, equals 2.5 percent of the $458 billion U.S. tax gap.[31] It's a pretty sure bet that once Uncle Sam wraps his arms around this new market, he will be collecting the taxes owed. Developing a tax strategy before you start trading is the best way to lower your tax bill.

While you may not be able to minimize your tax burden to zero without a very talented and expensive accountant, you should be conscious of your tax liabilities when trading and investing, lest it comes to bite you in the butt later on. At the height of the 2018 dump, many people had severe drawdowns on their trading accounts (buying bitcoin at 20k before it lost 80% of its price), and they technically owed money they didn't have. This is not a fun place to be.

The Crypto Tax Bite

Understandably, you may have confused the crypto economy libertarian ideals and call for voluntary taxes on crypto with the reality— Uncle Sam wants a bite of your crypto profits. Wasn't Bitcoin going to free us from the chains of government, taxes included? Why pay

---

31 IRS, "2018 Public Report," *IRS.gov*, https://www.irs.gov/pub/irs-pdf/p5315.pdf.

taxes at all? Keep in mind that change is incremental and Bitcoin has come a long way. While taxes are necessary, you can think of paying taxes as taking two steps forward and one step back. As long as you're smart about your investments, you can still make a profit on them, pay some tax and not lose all your money in the process.

There are a lot of grey zones in crypto right now, globally. In the UK your crypto gains are tax free below a certain amount (around $20k USD). Japan views crypto as legal tender and it's taxed as capital gains under their progressive taxation model, capped at 55% (ouch!). Russia's tax rate is a flat 13%. Puerto Rico has no tax on crypto. Hong Kong has no capitals gains tax, which is one reason it's a financial capital of Asia and home to many exchanges. Of course, these laws are susceptible to change, if they haven't done so already.

The US, while seemingly strict, has actually come a long way in its regulation around the industry. The US tax law (as of now) taxes bitcoin held under one year as short term capital gains tax (pretty high) and if it's sold after one year, the much more reasonable longer capital gains tax. Laws may vary by state and country and I'm not a tax professional. Whatever you choose to do should be discussed with a professional.

Cryptocurrency Tax Tips

Here are some cryptocurrency tax tips, which will of course be applied differently in each jurisdiction. Dealing in cryptocurrency can trigger many taxable events. You will naturally tally your trading accounts to determine taxable capital gains and potential offset losses. But don't forget the tokens you received from airdrops or as rewards, any gains from exchanges across crypto and fiat, and mining profits. And if you made a profit trading a sword for a fantasy game token, that too is taxable.

There are important differences, though. Cryptocurrencies are not considered a currency but intangible property for tax purposes.

- As you tally your income for the year, remember to include gains and losses from cryptocurrency trading, mining and staking.
- Are you carrying unrealized losses from the rollercoaster in crypto volatility this year? Remember those losses can offset capital gains across your entire investment portfolio and reduce your taxes. Close those losing positions and harvest tax losses. These losses can be carried over to the next year.
- When deducting expenses, don't forget your mining equipment. If you can deduct investment interest and expenses do so.
- Your asset inventory should include any tokens you hold at their current value. For example, if you hold Ripple tokens for use in business transactions, tokens for a travel booking platform you use, and tokens from rewards won in games and gambling, all should be accounted for. With a plethora of token rewards being divvied out as incentives, it may seem like funny money, but it's not. Your tokens can be traded for fiat.
- Not sure what to do with all those tokens? Like reward points, you may forget about them and never spend them. If you have held them for the prescribed period, donate them to charity and get a tax deduction.
- HODL coins to avoid unnecessary trading. Many wallets provide instant exchange at the click of a mouse across different crypto and fiat currencies. But remember, these exchanges create taxable capital gains.
- In the US, cryptocurrency is classified as a property, and therefore not subject to the Wash Sale Rule, requiring traders not repurchase a security sold at a loss within 30 days. The tax man, however, may still come after you.

CHAPTER 7. YOUR RISK MANAGEMENT PLAN

- When you receive payment in cryptocurrency as an employee or consultant, that income is still taxable.

If you keep in mind that virtual currency is taxed like real money, the tax man will not be chasing you.

Useful Links: I've included a list of useful links in my email list which you can download here:

> https://mishayurchenko.me/crypto-resources/

WHICH CRYPTO WALLET IS BEST?

Bad news typically gets more press than good news, and we are more apt to remember and share the bad stuff. So the news that over $1 billion was stolen in cryptocurrency in 2018, quadruple the amount of 2017, understandably has you concerned about how to keep your crypto safe.[32] Almost all of these thefts involved exchanges while only a few wallets were hacked. In South Korea, for example, seven exchanges but only 158 wallets were hacked in 2018.

Like many cryptocurrency investors, you may have started out with an exchange wallet. You have followed my guide (or, so I hope) and your crypto wallet value is rising. After hearing about the theft of $530 million worth of tokens from Coincheck in Japan and $195 million robbed from BitGrail, you understandably begin to get a bit antsy. Crime is more prevalent on cryptocurrency exchanges without anti-money laundering (AML) compliance standards. By choosing an exchange with lax regulatory standards, you may be assuming higher risk.

---

32 CipherTrace, "2018 Q3 Cryptocurrency Anti-Money Laundering Report," https://ciphertrace.com/wp-content/uploads/2018/10/crypto_aml_report_2018q3.pdf.

Meanwhile, I was calmly sipping a glass of cabernet and researching my next cryptocurrency investments safe in the knowledge that my coins were securely stored in my cryptocurrency wallet. By taking the time to buy a secure wallet you, too, can have peace of mind.

Wallet Features to Look For

Before you can choose a wallet, you need to determine which features you require—not all cryptocurrency wallets are alike. Here are the criteria I used to find a secure wallet with all the features I need.

Security—Security should be your number one priority. Has this brand of wallet ever experienced security hacks? How long has it been on the market? How many people use it?

User-friendliness—Especially for those new to the cryptocurrency world, private vs public keys, hot vs cold wallets, and other concepts will be confusing. A friend of mine opened a new free wallet before the Bitcoin Cash split, deposited $50 in bitcoin and waited for his Bitcoin Cash drop. But there was no free money for this investor. He cannot find the private key he copied somewhere and is clueless on how to recover his wallet. Review how the wallet works in advance. Research if, and how, a private key can be retrieved if you lose it.

Convenience—A client of mine took a day to send me some bitcoin last week. He said his bitcoin wallet was "very difficult" to access. I did not ask...but I imagined a hard wallet locked in a safe, in a fortified building with guards, in a remote location accessible only by drones. The crypto you use as disposable income should be in a wallet that is easily and quickly accessible. For long-term storage, more secure hardware wallet solutions exist (see below).

CHAPTER 7. YOUR RISK MANAGEMENT PLAN

Cost—Many suitable wallets are available for free, so shop around. Hardware wallets can range from $30 to hundreds of dollars.

Multi-cryptocurrency—Time was only two years when many investors dealt mainly in bitcoin, but if, like many investors, you're investing in other tokens—Ethereum, Ripple or any of the alt tokens, you will need a multi-currency wallet.

Multi-factor identification—Two-factor identification is a popular security feature. With the addition of biometrics, three-factor identification wallets are being introduced.

Multi-signature wallets—By using more than one private key, multi-signatures make a wallet harder to hack and easier to access if you lose a key. For example a wallet with five signatures may be accessible with any three of the signatures.

Built-in exchange—A wallet that seamlessly converts from crypto-fiat and crypto-crypto is a convenient feature. Some free wallets offer this service.

Software Wallets

Many investors will find their digital assets will be safe and easily accessible in a software wallet. Software wallets come in desktop, mobile and web-based versions. Though, be aware, software wallets have been hacked more often than hardware wallets. Your software wallet can only be accessed by your private key. Ensure it is stored where it cannot be accessed by others.

Hardware Wallets

Hardware wallets plug into your computer's USB device. Download the software to your computer, and you're ready to send or deposit cryptocurrency. Your private key is stored on a chip on the device where hackers, malware and viruses cannot access it. While setting up your device, you will be provided with random seed words to recover your wallet if it is stolen or broken.

Each wallet offers unique features. At this early stage, though, you may be trading an established reputation for security for fancy features. The new wallets are adding impressive functionality. The Atomic software wallet supports over 300 coins and atomic swaps. Exodus is popular for its in-built exchange. Hardware wallets are getting sleeker in design and features. HooFoo, which uses fingerprint and face identification, connects to your mobile device with a QR code. Then there are some less sexy wallets such as Trezor that are widely used and have an ironclad reputation for never having had a security breach.

Part II
37 STRATEGIES TO PROFIT IN THE NEW CRYPTO ECONOMY

"We keep moving forward, opening new doors, and doing new things, because we're curious and curiosity keeps leading us down new paths."
—WALT DISNEY

PART II. 37 STRATEGIES TO PROFIT IN THE NEW CRYPTO ECONOMY

I've outlined dozens of strategies that you can try out for yourself with step-by-step directions and links. I will caution you that tech is changing quickly, varies highly across countries, and needs to be independently assessed for your individual situation. I hope that you play around and experiment, and let these serve as starting points for deeper research. Some are highly experimental. Proceed with excitement and caution.

The original list includes links to various websites and resources for each strategy. To have this list emailed to you, visit

https://mishayurchenko.me/crypto-resources/

1. AIRDROPS

The saying *nothing is free in this world* was true, until blockchain startups started distributing their tokens at no charge. Airdrops, the free distribution of tokens by a blockchain project, are the easiest and cheapest way to add cryptocurrencies to your investment portfolio. The only requirement is that you have a specified token in your wallet and/or are a community member.

Why would a blockchain project distribute cryptocurrency for free? Airdrops are an effective marketing strategy. Blockchain projects can quickly build a community of investors and participants on their platforms by giving away free tokens. If you have free tokens to a peer-to-peer travel booking site, gaming platform, or money transfer service, you're more likely to try out the service. Watch for these opportunities to get free tokens in airdrops:

- ICO airdrops drop coins before the initial coin offering (ICO).
- Holder airdrops distribute coins to existing holders of the token.

- Hard forks distribute coins to holders of the tokens of the blockchain being forked. For example, Holders of Bitcoin on August 1, 2017 received Bitcoin Cash in a 1:1 token distribution.

The number of airdrops is expected to increase. More blockchains are raising money through private equity, and consequently missing out on the marketing benefits of an ICO. Airdrops are a way of promoting a startup to the wider investment community. For example, Dfinity raised over $100 million through major venture capital funds instead of a high profile public ICO. The decentralized cloud server followed up with the largest airdrop in history of 3.5 million tokens earlier this year to develop a network of users and liquidity in its token.

How to set it up:
1. Follow airdrop lists and sign up for notifications at Airdrop Alert, TopICOlist or similar services.
2. Ensure you have some coins in the required cryptocurrencies in your wallet and/or complete the required social media tasks (see *Tips* below).
3. Sign up on the company's website or through a website specializing in airdrops. Some airdrop websites will ask you to submit identification as part of the KYC/AML process.
4. Provide your cryptocurrency wallet address and wait for your new tokens to be deposited. Some airdrops will require the use of specific wallets.

Tips:
- Truth is, few things are actually free in life. More airdrops are following the bounty model and asking for a few marketing tasks before dropping your tokens, such as referring friends, or sharing and following the ICO on social media.

2. AFFILIATE INCOME

Affiliate income is one of the most popular ways to make passive income. Cryptocurrency affiliate programs pay you for making referrals who engage in the required action on a website—such as making a purchase or registering for a service. On blockchain platforms where amplifying network effects is key to increasing traffic and revenue, affiliate programs are generous. Referral commissions range from 10 to 75 percent. Even more money can be made when commissions are offered on second and third tier referrals. When your referrals make referrals, you also earn a percentage on the revenue generated.

You will be eligible for the referral fee once your referral engages in the required action. Here are examples of referral opportunities that could be earning you passive income:

- BitBond and XCoins pay 50 percent commission instantly when a lender you refer completes a loan transaction. XCoins pays a second tier fee of 3 percent on your referral's referrals.
- If you always fancied a career as a headhunter, Blockchaindevelopers. net will pay you $1,000 for any developer you refer and its clients subsequently hire.
- Refer farmers to the food and agricultural marketplace Foodcoin Ecosystem and receive 5 percent of all sales and advertising revenue.

ICO referrals are among the most active referral opportunities. Lists of top paying affiliate programs are regularly published online.

How to set it up:
1. Sign up for the affiliate program on the sponsoring website. Provide your cryptowallet address and fill out KYC/AML information.

2. Obtain the affiliate links from the sponsoring site (called referral URLs) to embed in your social media and blog, website and other content.
3. When someone clicks on the referral link and performs the required task, you will receive a commission.

Some tracking links may ask you to fill out a form, or tracking may be activated automatically when you embed the link in your content. These are the links that track the referrals that go to your referred partner's webpage, order form, and so on.

1. Click on Referral Tracking Links
2. Fill out the form information, as requested. For example:
    - Referral program
    - Webpage
    - Referral code

Tips:
- While many affiliates will continuously pay out as long as the referred customer does business on their platform, other payment programs are limited, and may be one time. Payout frequency can vary from daily to monthly. Be sure to check the terms.

3. REFERRAL REVENUE–EXCHANGES/WALLET SIGNUPS

New cryptocurrency exchanges and wallets are being launched daily. They want your business and they are willing to pay you for it. Generous sign-up bonuses are offered but the real money is in affiliate referrals. You can generate passive income by referring others. As the competition intensifies, the affiliate program payouts are increasing. The popular Trezo affiliate program has doubled the percentage of revenues you will be paid from 10 to 20 percent when your referrals use its crypto hard wallet. Competitor Ledger Nano S pays 10 percent for life.

When reviewing the offerings of exchanges or wallets, weighing the referral opportunities could help fill your wallet with passive income streams. Typically, when you lose money trading on an exchange you have to cut your losses. Even if you have a bad trading day, the potential exists to profit from referrals you make to your favorite trading platform. Most of the 100-plus cryptocurrency exchanges competing for your trading business offer referral programs. At leading exchange Coinbase, both you and your referral will receive a one-time $10 payment if your referral trades at least $100 within 180 days of registration. XCoins pays 25 percent on referrals and 5 percent on second tier referrals. Refer a friend to CFD exchange Plus500 and earn $700 after your referral spends $100.

How to set it up:
1. Sign up for the affiliate program on the sponsoring website. Provide your cryptowallet address and fill out KYC/AML information, if required.
2. Obtain the affiliate links from the sponsoring site (called referral URLs) to embed in your social media and blog, website and other content.
3. When someone clicks on the referral link and performs the required task (e.g., registers on an exchange and trades xx dollars, signs up for a wallet), you will receive a commission.

4. ICO BOUNTIES

Your blog, YouTube, Twitter, Reddit, Telegram and other social media accounts could be earning you money by helping blockchain startups promote their ICOs. ICO bounty programs provide an opportunity to earn tokens by performing various tasks. Bounties originated in the software community where software developers regularly provide rewards in exchange for finding bugs and security leaks in their code. ICO bounties are also given for software debugging but by far the largest demand is for marketing and promotional tasks that help attract investors in an ICO. In exchange, you will receive tokens in the ICO. Bitcoin, ether and even cash may be rewarded.

Bounties vary in terms of the degree of your resources required (typically, your time generating and sharing social media content). A few tokens can be earned by sharing ICO news on your Twitter, Instagram or other social media account, or making referrals to ICO Telegram and other social media groups. You may be asked to follow the platform's Instagram, Telegram or LinkedIn site. If you make a video profiling an ICO, you could make in the range of $50 to $1,000, depending on the quality of the video and the amount of traffic it generates.

How to set it up:
1. Visit a bounty hunting platform to find bounty tasks that could benefit from your talent and resources. The most popular are the BountyOx Network and ICOBountyHunt.
2. Carefully follow the bounty task instructions (e.g., Tweet three times a day for two weeks on ABC blockchain platform using only the phrasing provided on the website).
3. Submit evidence of the completed tasks carefully following the submission instructions.

Tips:
- Ensure you follow the content development instructions verbatim. Tweeting 29 times instead of 30, or writing a 450-word blog instead of 500 words (even if it receives 20k viewers) could disqualify you from receiving tokens.

- Ensure you follow the submission instructions verbatim as well. A transportation network DApp, for example, has three submission requirements: *After finishing your article/video/post paste the link in the discussion and in the bitcointalk bounty thread and submit it.* You need to complete all three to earn the bounty.

5. SECURITY TOKEN OFFERINGS (INVEST IN OR LAUNCH AN STO)

Choosing a security token offering (STO) over an initial coin offering (ICO) could help you earn more. Both fundraising methods sell a stake in a Blockchain startup in the form of cryptocurrency tokens. Though raising money through an ICO is becoming more challenging due to concerns over the quality of these unregistered securities. Close to 50 percent of ICOs failed in 2017, and the failure rate is rising. The startups that do succeed are raising more money. The money is flowing to fewer but higher quality issues.

A fundamental difference is that an STO must be backed by the assets, profits or revenues of a blockchain business. Importantly, STOs comply with securities regulations which, in the US and some other jurisdictions, ICOs are also now required to do. Keep in mind that ICOs which circumvent US listings to avoid complying with securities laws are more likely to be low quality issues. I go into STOs in more detail in Part 3.

How to set it up:
1. Review STO instead of ICO offerings online. Follow upcoming offerings at STOCheck or STOpedia.
2. Before investing, check the STO rating and read any related analyst reports. ICORatings.com rates STOs.

3. Determine if you qualify as an investor for this offering. The STO has filed for securities registration exemption under rule 506(c). These STOs still must comply with securities regulation but don't have to submit in-depth investment prospectuses. Exempt STOs are mainly open to accredited institutional investors—those with income of more than $200k or a net worth in excess of $1 million.
4. Follow the STO investment registration process on the company website (KYC, AML, wallet registration etc.). KYC/AML verification is required to be placed on the white list of accredited investors.

Tips:
- You can trade security tokens in the same way you can trade ICO tokens or company shares. There is a 12-month lock up period, though, before you can exchange STOs in the secondary market. Security tokens are currently traded on at least a dozen exchanges.[33]
- These exchanges should have a white list verification process to ensure your counterparties are accredited investors.

6. DIVIDENDS

Investors love dividends because they provide a steady stream of passive income. Dividends distribute a percentage of the profits of a company to shareholders at regular intervals, typically quarterly for stocks. Like public companies, some Blockchain DApps pay dividends to their token holders—tokens in DApps are the equivalent of shares in a company.

In addition to the dividend payments, based on the past performance of dividend-paying stocks, your tokens could earn higher returns. In the

---

33 Maverick SA, "Discovering the 11 Exchanges Ready, or Almost Ready, to Host STO," *Medium.com*, https://medium.com/@MavericSA/discovering-the-11-exchanges-ready-or-almost-ready-to-host-sto-9b03be8e9c71.

stock market, dividend paying stocks outperform non-dividend payers over the long term and are less volatile. The superior performance has been attributed to these companies more efficiently managing income, which ensures reliable dividend payments. Moreover, investors who reinvest their dividends significantly outperform those who don't.

Dividends paid out in cryptocurrency tokens could provide an even stabler revenue stream. Stock dividends can be withheld at the discretion of the company board, which may also change the amount of the dividend. Crypto dividend payments, on the other hand, are coded into the cryptocurrency protocol. The dividend could still be adjusted based on preset criteria, but generally without human intervention dividend payments are automatically paid out and thus more reliable.

How the dividends are calculated, however, varies greatly across cryptocurrencies. The cryptocurrency world has been very innovative in developing dividend structures. KuCoin distributes 50 percent of the trading fees daily among those with KuCoin in their wallet. Digix Gold Token pays a percentage of the transaction fees in dividends. The majority of crypto dividends use a proof-of-stake model, which is similar to the corporate dividend model. Wallet holders receive a proportionate amount of the rewards and fees for verifying transactions to the amount of coins they have staked.

How to set it up:
1. Review lists with the Top Proof of Stake Cryptocurrencies to familiarize yourself with the opportunities available. Less popular coins will provide more affordable staking opportunities.
2. Buy the coin through the ICO or on an exchange.
3. Watch your dividend streams roll into your crypto wallet. To compound your earnings, reinvest your dividends by buying more tokens.

Tips:
- Ensure the exchange and wallet you're using pay and accept dividends. NEO gas dividends, for example, are only paid out on the Kucoin and Binance exchanges.
- Check to see if the coin has a lock-in period before it pays out dividend (check the resources online for more links)

7. TRADING BOTS

Trading bots are designed to give you an advantage in fast moving currency trading markets. These automated trading programs can engage in more complex and faster trades than you could manually. In cryptocurrency markets operating 24/7, they are indispensable tools for managing your open trades while you sleep.

Trading bots execute buy and sell orders based on preprogrammed instructions. They provide basic stop/loss and take profit orders, real time pricing, and technical analysis tools and charts. More advanced features such as backtesting—to test and refine your strategies—may be provided. Some trading bots do one thing very well such as ArbitrageBot, which takes the opposite trading positions across different crypto exchanges to profit from differences in prices; or Telegram Assistant, which takes trade orders via the popular messaging system. While others such as Haasbot and Tradewave provide a comprehensive selection of trading and technical analysis tools across major exchanges.

If you have a winning trading strategy, consider developing your own trading bot. If you can provide traders an edge, you could make a lot of money. The leading crypto trading programs sell monthly subscriptions, providing a steady recurring income stream. For non-programmers, many freelance programmers with experience creating trading programs are available for hire.

How to set it up:
1. Start with reviews of the most profitable cryptocurrency trading bots to familiarize yourself with their functionality and pricing. Some are free while advanced programs can cost thousands of dollars a month.
2. Make a list of the features you need and would like. If you're new to crypto trading, copy trading is a good way to familiarize yourself with cryptocurrency trading strategies and tools.
3. Many programs can be tested with limited functionality. Paper trade while experimenting with different trading bots.
4. With monthly subscriptions using stepped pricing, you can explore a program in more detail and graduate with experience to expert features.

Tips:
- Cryptocurrency trading bots is a young, active area of development. Avoid locking into a system long term as the competition changes daily.

8. MINING

If you have read the news headlines *Bitcoin Mining Is No Longer Profitable!*, you may have abandoned the idea of becoming a crypto miner. Like any business venture, as competition increases profitability declines, but don't write off mining as a potential investment. Cryptocurrencies have a strong motivation to ensure miners are rewarded for doing necessary mining work. Mining is the process through which cryptocurrency transactions are verified and recorded. By distributing this processing work amongst individual computers, the overhead of large centralized e-commerce processors such as a PayPal or Amazon is eliminated.

Cryptocurrency miners are facing declining profitability owing to increases in computing power demands and the complexity of the cryptographic puzzles solved to verify transactions. Fortunately for miners, the developers of cryptocurrencies have a strong incentive to ensure mining is profitable enough to attract enough miners to do essential mining work.

Existing mining protocols are being reworked to ensure miners are adequately incentivized (the proof-of-work protocol used by Bitcoin and Ethereum is being upgraded to a proof-of-stake protocol), while new cryptocurrencies are developing new protocols and incentive mechanisms to attract miners. In fact, cryptocurrencies are competing with incentives to attract miners.

How to set it up:
1. Refer to a cryptocurrency mining calculator to compare potential mining profitability scenarios based on hashing power, power consumption, electricity cost per kwh and the pooling fee. A miner paying 19 cents per kilowatt hour in Tokyo, Japan will have higher costs than a miner paying 8 cents/kWh in hydro-powered Vancouver, Canada.
2. Buy your mining hardware. ASIC miners are the preferred workhorses of Bitcoin miners owing to their fast processing capacity and power efficiency.
3. Download mining software for your OS (Mac, Windows, Linux).
4. Join a mining pool. Together with other miners, you will process the transactions for one block (Bitcoin has about 1 megabyte of data per block).

5. Receive a share of the block reward based on the computing power you have contributed. The largest mining pools charge fees between 1–3 percent.

The value of mining equipment quickly depreciates as higher performing ASICs are introduced. Cloud mining and staking are ways to mine without investing in equipment (see below). Buyer beware: Many unprofitable cloud mining opportunities are being offered in the market.

9. STAKING

Staking is a form of mining whereby those with the most coins stake a node on a mining network and process a new block of transactions. Under the proof-of-stake (POS) protocol, the mining work (validating and recording transactions) is randomly assigned to miners on the network. The staker can mine transactions equal to the value of the coins staked by a mining pool. If the value of your coins is equal to 2 percent of the coins on the network, then you will earn a mining fee of 2 percent of the total transactions on the network.

Staking is a form of dividend. NEO, Dash, and OkCash are part of a growing pool of cryptocurrencies choosing to use the POS in place of the proof of work (POW) consensus mechanism.

NEO stakes can expect to receive 5.5 percent of the value of their stake in new coins. Microtransaction coin OkCash is paying 10 percent of the value of the stake. Some coins have high minimums (e.g., Dash 1,000 coins) to stake a wallet.

Under POW mining, in contrast, the miner with the highest performing computing equipment is most likely to make a profit. The risk is

PART II. 37 STRATEGIES TO PROFIT IN THE NEW CRYPTO ECONOMY

higher of an entity behind these powerful computers gaining control of 51 percent of the hashing power and thus control over the validation and reversal of transactions.

A risk of staking is the devaluation of your coins during the staking process. While the block is being processed, your staked coins are bound to the staking node. If prices fall during this period, you will be unable to sell them.

How to Set It Up:
1. Buy coins in the token you want to stake. Tokens can be bought during the ICO and on exchanges.
2. Download the staking software and wallet for the coin to stake.
3. Follow the instructions to move the coins from the wallet to the staked node (often a click on, or cut-and-paste of, the staking address).

Tips:
- You don't have a large enough share in a coin to stake a node but would like to profit from staking? Proof of Stake.io is one of the new platforms pooling coins and allowing individuals to stake as part of a pool.

10. CRYPTO FAUCETS

Crypto faucets are a way of earning crypto—but don't quit your day job! Cryptocurrency faucets are a way of making micro-earnings in exchange for performing small tasks. You may be asked to complete captchas, solve puzzles, or simply click on a website page. For a full day's work, you may make a dollar or two. But before you can withdraw your money, you need to meet a limit, the time required to meet the limits set by some faucet sites may not be a practical use of your hours.

PART II. 37 STRATEGIES TO PROFIT IN THE NEW CRYPTO ECONOMY

Your micro-earnings are paid in satoshis—one hundred millionth of a bitcoin (0.00000001 BTC). Loyalty and referral bonuses are also offered. You may even earn while playing games, although many games will entice you in and then require you to pay to continue playing. Faucets make money by driving traffic to advertisements on their website. It is not uncommon to face many ads before being able to perform a task. If after five clicks you're still in an infinite advertising loop, consider whether it is a good investment of your time.

How to set it up:
1. Sign up for a wallet such as faucet.io that aggregates satoshis. This service will allow you to withdraw in larger amounts.
2. Register on the faucet websites you want to participate in.
3. Conduct the required tasks and earn satoshis!

Tips:
- Faucet websites come and go. Of the faucets on one top 10 Bitcoin faucet list, one third have closed.

11. STEEM.IO BLOGGING

If you're not hanging out on Steemit, you may soon become a social media dinosaur. Savvy bloggers and Youtubers who are sharing their content on the Steemit social media network are reaping generous rewards. Steemit not only pays some of the highest earnings to content producers and curators but the social network has designed its reward system to also provide rewards for the quality of the post, called SteamPower. So far, Steemit has paid out $43 million to its close to one million bloggers.

The main ways to earn on Steemit are writing, commenting on and upvoting posts, and receiving upvotes for your posts. Three types of cryptocurrencies are paid:

- Steem Dollars (SDB) can be used to promote posts.
- Steem Power is a measure of your influence on Steemit. The more Steem Power you have the more you earn.
- STEEM—Steem Power, an internal token, can be converted into the STEEM token, which can be traded for other crypto and fiat currencies.

Seventy-five percent of a post's earnings go to the writer. Twenty-five percent of the SDB earned by a post is distributed among curators in the form of Steem Power. Your share of the SP will be weighted based on timing and your current steam power.

According to Steemit blogger *liberosist*, the money your content generates depends on:

1. *Eventual popularity of the post (Total SBD generated)*
2. *Your Steem Power (Your stake in the Steem pie)*
3. *Timing of your vote (How soon after the post was made)*
4. *Your Voting Power (How often you upvote)*

In two years, *liberosist* has earned $1,884 writing content on how to make money on Steem. This may not seem like a lot, and it isn't, but we're in the early stages and as we all know network effects can be explosive once there are enough users (think about the first lonely users of Facebook or Kindle books).

PART II. 37 STRATEGIES TO PROFIT IN THE NEW CRYPTO ECONOMY

How to set it up:
1. Sign up for a Steemit account. Write your *introduce yourself* tag and post your photo. Provide the link to your Steemit profile on your other social media accounts.
2. Before posting, research the tags and note which ones have high volume and are trending.
3. When posting, choose the allocation of Steem Power Dollars vs Steem Power you prefer—50/50 is the default. The more Steem Power you earn the higher your STEEM earnings.
4. Remember, you can also earn by commenting and upvoting on other posts.
5. Transfer Steem Power to the STEEM token to convert and withdraw your earnings.

Tip:
- Steem Power is determined by a number of factors, including whether or not your vote reflects the majority voter sentiment and how many upvotes you provide in a day. If you upvote more than 40 posts a day, your Steem Power value could fall below 50 percent.
- The Steemit system can be confusing. The best way to understand it is to become a Steemer and start posting and commenting.

12. EARN.COM

Earn crypto through answering emails.

The blockchain is giving control of data back to consumers. Instead of middlemen making money off of your data, you can sell it directly to marketers. The direct sales channel provides the opportunity to sell more specific data at higher fees. earn.com has taken advantage of this more personalized data market by aggregating consumers whose profile and information are in very high demand by marketers.

Founder Balaji S. Srinivasan, a serial entrepreneur and Stanford alum, has basically put his contacts on the earn.com digital ledger and invited friends and others to join. The result is a highly targeted site of curated business professionals with a focus on the cryptocurrency and blockchain space. In exchange for a fee, these professionals provide their sought-after opinions to marketers by answering emails and filling out surveys.

Earn pays higher fees than many other data aggregation platforms, although the process to join is stricter. Members represent 95 targeted groups including cryptocurrency funds, venture funds, ICO investors, digital currency investors, social media users and software engineers and developers. Several Stanford University groups are also featured. You can choose how much you charge for answering an email—$1, $5, $20 or $100. Advertisers are willing to pay you higher fees because they receive response rates of 30-70 percent within 24 hours versus 1.7 percent for typical marketing surveys. As an added bonus, some of these emails lead to business opportunities. Headhunters, for example, asking about the programming skill set and work availability of earn.com software developers also recruit from the exclusive community.

How to set it up:
1. Create an earn.com profile and link your LinkedIn account for verification.
2. Choose how much you will charge for answering an email—$1, $5, $20 or $100.
3. Select the groups you want to be a part of from the list. Each will ask for some form of verification.
4. Wait for emails to be sent. Perform the required task (an email or survey) by the deadline.

5. Your fee will be automatically deposited in your wallet. You may also choose to donate your earnings to charity.

Tip:
- Don't forget to check off the box to receive Airdrops—a new feature added in January 2018. earn.com will provide you notice of ICO airdrops that have chosen to market to this curated group of blockchain developers and investors.
- Earn up to $100 more by earning $1 in bitcoin for each verified friend you refer to earn.com. Also, note that you need to have some sort of tech expertise—either working for a tech company or holding a senior position in one (or be a developer).

13. PURSE.IO

The often-quoted maxim *Buy Low, Sell High* used to be a sure way to make money. But as e-commerce fees have risen from 10 to 30–50 percent, the middleman is often the only one who profits. Peer-to-peer trading over the decentralized blockchain with low or no commissions is making this basic sales model profitable again. purse.io is one of the new e-commerce channels leveraging P2P trading and cryptocurrencies to provide shoppers on Amazon cheaper goods.

If you have Amazon rewards you're not using, why not buy something on Amazon for someone else at a discount, or use your digital currency to buy Amazon goods at a discount.

How to set it up:
1. Register on the purse.io website. The shopping process varies based on the discount you seek. You can obtain a larger discount if you're willing to wait longer for the delivery of your goods.

PART II. 37 STRATEGIES TO PROFIT IN THE NEW CRYPTO ECONOMY

2. If you would like a 5 percent discount:
   - Submit an order for the Amazon item you would like to buy.
   - purse.io will fulfill the order and deliver it within two to five days.

3. If you would like a 6-33 percent discount:
   - The buyer submits his/her wish list of Amazon goods to purse.io.
   - purse.io will match the buyer with an earner with Amazon gift cards.
   - The earner with unused Amazon reward points buys the Amazon good on behalf of the buyer.
   - Then, the earner sells the good to the buyer at their desired discount in exchange for digital currency.

14. FREELANCE FOR CRYPTOCURRENCY

Freelance and get paid in cryptocurrencies. A big advantage of peer-to-peer job boards is you get to take home most, if not all, of your pay. Ethlance charges no fees. The top freelance website Upwork, in contrast, is currently taking 20 percent of your first $500 earned per client, 10 percent of the next $500-$10,000, and 5 percent of anything over $10,000. Since they don't accept cryptocurrency, if you do accept a payment in cryptocurrency off of the site, you could lose your site privileges. Nonetheless, you can still find a large number of freelance crypto assignments on Upwork paying in fiat currency.

Many of the freelance jobs paying in cryptocurrency are listed by blockchain startups. All the major freelance skills are in demand— software developers, web designers, translators, marketers, writers, and so on.

The freelancing market for cryptocurrency is taking off more slowly than the general crypto job boards, which are burgeoning with current job offers. The listed jobs on some freelance websites are two months old. Be patient. The growing workforce accepting permanent jobs in cryptocurrency will be sure to turn to crypto freelance jobs platforms when they need temporary help.

How to set it up:
1. Visit freelance websites advertising jobs paying in cryptocurrency.
2. Post your profile and photo.
3. Take any relevant job skills tests, if offered.
4. Offer to do a few jobs at a reduced rate to develop a portfolio and rating.

Peruse these job boards for the latest offerings:

- Ethlance — This zero fee platform pays in ether.
- Blocklancer — The Fiverr of Ethereum. Tell your future clients what you will do for ether.
- cryptogrind.com — This site pays in bitcoin stored in multisig wallets.
- Cryptocurrency jobs — A freelance marketplace matching freelancers with jobs with blockchain startups.
- Coinality — A job board aggregating all jobs paying in cryptocurrency.

Tips:
- Also check out job boards on Reddit, such as r/Jobs4Bitcoins

PART II. 37 STRATEGIES TO PROFIT IN THE NEW CRYPTO ECONOMY

15. LENDING FOR MARGIN TRADING

Having an unprofitable trading day? On cryptocurrency exchanges, you still have the opportunity to end the day *in the black* (trading parlance for *profitable*). On the Poloniex, Bitfinex, and Kraken exchanges, for instance, your potential to make money does not only depend on your trading performance. You can also make money on interest from margin loans you lend to other traders. Exchanges provide margin loans to traders allowing them to trade more than they have in their account. On the decentralized blockchain, peers can provide direct margin loans to other peers at low rates.

Margin borrowers assume more risk when they trade on margin. You may have heard of stories of margin traders losing lots of money. Using financial leverage not only amplifies the amount of money you can win but also your losses. The lender, in contrast, has low risk because the borrower provides you with security. The money in the trader's cash account serves as collateral for the margin account. Demand for loans will be higher on exchanges with higher volume.

How to set it up:
1. Sign up to a cryptocurrency exchange that supports peer-to-peer margin lending.
2. When choosing an exchange consider:
   - What is the risk profile of the lender you will accept? Will you choose an exchange that only allows accredited investors to trade on margin? Or one that allows all traders margin accounts?
   - Are you willing to lend to a trader who assumes a conservative 2:1 leverage or higher risk 4:1 leverage? You want to avoid an exchange that provides 100:1 leverage.

PART II. 37 STRATEGIES TO PROFIT IN THE NEW CRYPTO ECONOMY

3. Open a lending account. This account is in addition to the standard trading and margin accounts.
4. Indicate which coins you're willing to lend and how much you will lend.

Tips:
- Compare lending rates. Some exchanges may require you to lend out at least $10,000 to make any money from margin lending.

16. ACT AS A BITCOIN BROKER

A cryptocurrency broker arranges trades between buyers and sellers for a fee. As a broker, you will make money from the difference between the bid and ask price. Unlike the mature foreign exchange markets in which the spreads are super thin, brokers can benefit from wider spreads across cryptocurrencies. For the potentially higher returns, though, you will face more risk.

The biggest risks you will face as a cryptocurrency broker are price risk, counterparty risk and liquidity risk. Price volatility in cryptocurrencies is high, though it is declining. Large and frequent price swings not only provide the opportunity to make huge profits but also incur large losses. Black swan events—unexpected events that cause large price spikes—are harder to predict in the nascent crypto markets but more common.

Counterparty risk is high and some exchanges have lax trader verification processes. In many tokens, you will have few trading partners. Liquidity risk is the risk you will not be able to find a trading partner to take the other side of a trade. Liquidity is good in the top 10 coins by market capitalization (Bitcoin, Ether, Ripple etc.) but is thin in many

PART II. 37 STRATEGIES TO PROFIT IN THE NEW CRYPTO ECONOMY

coins. After familiarizing yourself with the risks and developing a risk management plan, you're ready to set up a virtual brokerage.

How to set it up:
1. Check with a lawyer to verify if you need a license to be a cryptocurrency broker in the jurisdictions you're trading in.
2. Register with the exchanges you want to trade on.
3. Consider using a trading bot such as Haasbot that connects to many major exchanges and provides a single screen view of all your positions.
4. Advertise as a seller and/or buyer on the exchanges you do business on. Some exchanges will have a minimum deposit requirement to advertise as a market maker.
5. Set out your trading terms. Do you require counterparties to be KYC/AML verified? Do you have special conditions/trading limits for new counterparties?
6. Cite the payment methods you will accept (bank transfer, credit card, wire transfer, Skrill, OKPay).

Tip:
- Some exchanges such as LocalBitcoins strictly prevent you from brokering, that is buying and selling Bitcoin on behalf of others. Not to despair. DApps such as Birake make it easy for you to set up your own exchange and trade across many crypto exchanges.

17. WORK FOR A CRYPTO/BLOCKCHAIN COMPANY AND EARN SALARY IN BITCOIN

Working for crypto is becoming easier. Cryptocurrency job boards are connecting tens of thousands of professionals to jobs that pay in cryptocurrency. More jobs paying in digital currency are popping up on traditional job boards like indeed.com. Blockchain job positions

PART II. 37 STRATEGIES TO PROFIT IN THE NEW CRYPTO ECONOMY

doubled in 2017. If crypto is not offered as a payment currency, don't hesitate to try and negotiate crypto payments as part of your salary package. Whether the salary is in crypto or fiat, the native tokens and options on tokens of the employer may be thrown in as an incentive.

Most jobs paying in crypto are related to blockchain technology and ICO platform development and marketing. Industries are advertising for software and database developers and engineers to integrate the digital ledger into their transaction management in financial services, supply chains and many other functions. ICO platforms require blockchain expertise to develop peer-to-peer platforms in financial services, gaming, hospitality, transportation, and many other areas.

How to set it up:
1. Search the cryptocurrency and standard job boards for the positions that interest you.
2. Click Apply and follow the application instructions.
3. Most jobs boards will offer to register your resume and keep it on file.

Popular cryptocurrency job boards include:

- CryptoJobsList
- Cryptocurrency Jobs https://cryptocurrencyjobs.co/
- CryptoJobs https://crypto.jobs/

18. LINKEDIN

LinkedIn is another good place to launch or advance your crypto career. All senior management professionals involved in the blockchain and cryptocurrency space use LinkedIn as their main business profile. They also choose to list positions they seek to fill via the leading professional business network. A quick perusal reveals over 800 cryptocurrency jobs listed in the US, 600 blockchain jobs in London, UK, and 100 blockchain developer jobs in Singapore. Here is how to get the attention of those with hiring authority on LinkedIn.

- Develop a LinkedIn profile. Check the footnotes for a free PDF guide.[34]
- Use keywords related to the job positions you want (e.g., blockchain developer, frontend blockchain developer, software engineer) to help recruiters find you.
- Ask employers and colleagues to provide you with references to include in your LinkedIn profile.
- Search and respond to LinkedIn job ads.
- Connect to people you know and want to be connected with to gain access to their network.
- Join LinkedIn groups in the industries and disciplines you want to work in.

In LinkedIn groups, 1.8 million people are seeking to make job connections in the Software and Technology subgroup Software & Technology Professionals: Managers | HR | Recruiters | Blockchain | Investors.

The Hub.Careers Blockchain subgroup has over 400,000 members.

Search under LinkedIn groups to find many other fintech/blockchain career groups of interest to you.

---

34 leisure Jobs, "LinkedIn The Ultimate Cheatsheet," https://www.leisurejobs.com/cheatsheet/ultimate-linkedin-cheat-sheet-A4.pdf.

PART II. 37 STRATEGIES TO PROFIT IN THE NEW CRYPTO ECONOMY

19. BITCOIN FORKS

Imagine waking up one morning and your bank balance has doubled—but alas, it was only a dream. In the cryptocurrency world that dream can come true through a process called forks—the creation of a new blockchain from a legacy blockchain. Forks are a method of updating a blockchain. To make changes to a blockchain, a consensus is required. When consensus is not achieved, a permanent split occurs and a new currency is created. Permanent forks can be a windfall for existing currency holders. If you're holding the legacy currency in a wallet at the time of the fork, you will automatically receive the new currency at a ratio of 1:1.

A major Bitcoin fork took place in August 2017 when the developers of Bitcoin Cash upgraded the blocks of the Bitcoin blockchain from 1 MB to 8 MB to improve the scalability and transaction processing speed of the network. Since a consensus was not reached on the upgrade, the new currency was created. A year after the fork, Bitcoin Cash was trading at $700USD. Bitcoin Gold (BTG), which hard forked almost a decade ago, was trading at a more modest $24 USD in October 2018—still a good return on free money.

How to set it up:
1. Sign up for email updates on the fork. Wait for the block at which the fork will take place to be announced.
2. Ensure you have the main currency in your wallet before the block is reached.
3. Ensure you have an authorized wallet. The Bitcoin Cash fork, for example, only deposited Bitcoin Cash into certain types of wallets listed on its website.
4. Wait for the new currency to be deposited into your wallet.

Tip:
- Ensure you have the legacy currency deposited in your wallet well in advance of the fork. The published estimated block date for the Bitcoin Cash fork was actually one day after the block was reached. Those who had not transferred Bitcoin into an authorized wallet on time missed out.

20. MAKE YOUR OWN CRYPTOCURRENCY TOKEN

This strategy is for all you entrepreneurs and developers out there. If you're using crypto tokens to transfer money, travel, play games and other activities, you appreciate the benefits of tokenized assets. Virtual money can be securely traded and tracked between parties anywhere in the world. A dollar printing machine can cost up to $50,000, but a digital mint on the blockchain allows anyone to create tokens. You can choose among a variety of DApps to help you make your own tokens.

A token is a digital currency used to facilitate decentralized peer-to-peer transactions. Most of the tokens issued to date run on the Ethereum blockchain enabling cross-compatibility across DApps using the ERC-20 protocol. Ethereum upgraded the Bitcoin blockchain by adding smart contract functionality, allowing businesses to program any function into self-executing contracts. Tokens activate these smart contract actions.

Blockchain startups issue and sell tokens to investors through initial coin offerings (ICO). Assuming you're going to do an ICO and sell your tokens to the public, here are the steps you need to take:

- If you're selling your token in the US or another jurisdiction that considers a token a security, register the token or apply for an

exemption. Consult a lawyer or ICO agency with legal services for assistance.
- Choose your branding and design.
- Develop your website, whitepaper and pitch deck.
- Develop your platform interface and smart contracts.
- Determine how your tokens will be distributed (e.g., founders, team, private investors, ICO, marketing and promotion, rewards, administration/operations). This distribution will be presented in the whitepaper.
- Add KYC/AML compliance to your registration process. You may choose to conduct this verification in-house or outsource it.
- Launch your social media and public relations campaign (Medium, Twitter, Reddit, blog, Youtube, Telegram). Produce and share lots of content to tell the world about your token.

Feeling overwhelmed? ICO agencies can help you through the process. There's also an app for that. DApps like Waves and Emotiq have developed platforms that make it easy, fast and less costly to create a token and smart contracts. Both boast smart contracts that can be created by non-programmers.

Tip: Securities regulators in the US, Japan and other jurisdictions are cracking down on ICOs. Depending on where you register, you may be required to register your token as a security or apply for an exemption. The extra compliance steps could pay off and help you sell more tokens. Wiser investors are placing money in ICOs with high ratings.

21. MAKE YOUR OWN CRYPTOCURRENCY COIN

If you're really ambitious, you can develop your own coin. An important difference between coins and tokens is tokens launch on existing blockchains whereas coins develop their own blockchain. Why develop a new blockchain? The Ethereum blockchain hosts 82.6 percent of tokens but transaction processing time and capacity limitations are keeping some businesses on the sidelines. Seeing a big opportunity, new blockchains offering performance improvements are being introduced.

Popular blockchain coins include Tezos, Waves, NEO, EOS, Litecoin and Ripple. Ripple saw an opportunity to develop a blockchain to meet the high volume transaction processing needs of large businesses. Targeting blockchain startups, Waves provides the speed of a centralized exchange with fast and cheap token and smart contract creation. Or you may build a blockchain focusing on niche apps such as gaming platforms. Competition is high and Ethereum is working on an upgrade to its popular network, but if you can build a better blockchain you could do well. New blockchain platforms dominate the top coin market capitalization rankings.

If you want to become the next EOS, Cardano or Tezos, here are the steps:

1. Identify your use case. What is the function of your Blockchain? What type of Dapps will you host?
2. Develop your consensus mechanism—the method by which your network will verify and record transactions.
3. Design your Blockchain architecture. Are you making upgrades to an existing blockchain (Ethereum, Hyperledger?), or starting from scratch?
4. Develop your APIs. Basic functions include keys and signatures; data authentication, storage and retrieval; smart contract functions (transactions, escrows).
5. Hire your programming team, or Blockchain developer freelancers on a crypto or other job site.

22. SELL YOUR PERSONAL DATA TO MARKETERS

The data flowing across your mobile phone apps is worth a lot to marketers but monetizing it is not easy. What if you could choose which information to sell, at what price and to whom? Welcome to the democratization of data—a marketing world in which the consumer owns the data. Two thirds of Korean mobile phone owners are already making money across their apps with an application called AirBloc https://airbloc.org/. Advertisers are willing to pay more money to buy your data directly because they can collect more precisely targeted personalized data. And on the blockchain, they can trace and track the data flows, thereby avoiding fake data and improving the quality of the data they buy.

Many dApps are introducing new ways for consumers to control and sell their data to marketers directly for cryptocurrency. You may not realize how much valuable data you own. humanity.co, for example, wants to give you data property rights over your healthcare information. Medical research, drug development and sales, and physician marketing are some of the markets willing to pay for your health data. Datum https://datum.org/ connects product managers with crypto enthusiasts.

How to set it up:
Choose the application you would like to use. Download the mobile app (if available) and follow the registration procedures. Here are a few apps worth a look:

1. AirBloc is one of many new blockchain Dapps helping consumers monetize their data. The AirBloc API works across many apps, allowing you to manage your data from one app. You decide which apps can use your data and which data to sell. A brilliant feature

of AirBloc is the ability to combine data across apps (e.g., your Facebook and Telegram accounts) and provide the marketer with more valuable data, for which you can charge a higher fee.
2. Wibson is a data intermediary that connects data buyer demands with you the data provider. The Wibson mobile app allows you to connect your social media accounts (currently Facebook) and location. You get paid in Wibson tokens for your data. Wibson uses notaries to audit data to improve data quality. Quality data is worth more.
3. You could earn some serious crypto if you deal in a specialized data market. Bottos' Datanno is a data market for the AI market, which has an insatiable appetite for data. By allowing anyone to share and sell AI data, Datanno plans to cut AI data costs and model training by as much as 30 percent, helping even small AI developers to be more competitive.

23. SELL YOUR GIFT CARDS FOR CRYPTO

Oh, no, another gift card in your stocking! Do most expire before you can use them? Why not sell your unused gift cards at a discount for cryptocurrency? Register and list your gift cards on a gift card site. Buyers need simply choose the gift cards they want and scan the QR code of their crypto wallet to complete the sale. You instantly receive payment in your crypto wallet.

Crypto card shops provide many savings incentives to buyers. You could even sell your gift card at par or a premium. Here's how. Currently, Nike is offering a $10 coupon to anyone who spends $50 on a Nike card on egifter.com Therefore, the value of your $50 Nike card is actually $60. Additionally, eGifter provides bitcoin rewards based on the amount of bitcoin a buyer spends on its site.

PART II. 37 STRATEGIES TO PROFIT IN THE NEW CRYPTO ECONOMY

How to set it up:
Visit these popular gift card sites and start exchanging:

1. Gift cards for all major American brands are available on egifter.com. Sell your unused Nordstrom, Dunkin Donuts or Nike gift cards at a discount in exchange for bitcoin.
2. Amazon, Nintendo, Uber and Walmart cards, and various Canadian homegrown brands are among the dozens of popular gift cards for sale on Canada's coincards.ca. Get paid in bitcoin, Litecoin, DASH, and other popular crypto coins.
3. Popular US exchange Coinbase now allows you to withdraw your cryptocurrency trading profits in gift cards. Using the Nike example above, you could then sell the card on a gift card exchange and make more money.

Tip:
- An even easier way to get crypto is to ask for a bitcoin gift card for your birthday—or a gift card for your favorite crypto gaming, esports or shopping platform. If you have your own altcoin, cryptcard.io makes custom gift cards.

24. INVEST IN CRYPTOCURRENCY ETFS

Have the wild price swings in cryptocurrencies left you standing on the sidelines? Exchange traded funds (ETFs) are the lowest risk way of investing in volatile cryptocurrencies. Cryptocurrency indexes and ETFs track an index or basket of cryptocurrencies or tokens. By spreading risk across a basket of cryptocurrencies, you can smooth out volatility and reduce your risk exposure. These passive investment strategies outperform active investing over the long term.

Passive funds avoid the high fees incurred by active investors trading in and out of assets, and therefore have low expense ratios. ETFs can be constructed to reflect low volatility, high dividend yield, strong past performance and many other factors. These flexible attributes can be applied to balance an investment portfolio.

The challenge is finding cryptocurrency ETFs to invest in. US regulators have turned down nine crypto ETF applications this year. And several Swiss ETFs were delisted in October 2018. You will not have to wait long, though, to reduce the volatility and smooth out earnings in your cryptocurrency portfolio. The launch of cryptocurrency ETFs is expected in 2019. ETFs most likely to get approval in the near term will be secured by physical assets.

How to set it up:
While waiting for the approval of cryptocurrency products, many cryptocurrency index funds are open for investment. Index funds like ETFs provide a low cost diversification and hedging strategy. How do they differ? An advantage of ETFs is that they can be traded like stocks throughout the day whereas indexes are mutual funds valued daily based on their underlying net asset value. Here is a mix of crypto ETFs to consider:

1. CRYPT020 https://crypto20.com/ was the first cryptocurrency token-as-a-fund.
2. US-based Coinbase and South Korean exchange Bithumb (Bithumb Market Index (BTMI) and Bithumb Altcoin Market Index (BTAI)) are among the exchanges to recently launch indexes.
3. Abra https://www.abra.com/blog/the-bit10/ has launched a token called the BIT10 that tracks the top 10 cryptocurrencies each month by market value. It may look and act like an ETF but Abra says it is a different investment instrument.

4. The Digital Asset Index Fund https://www.digitalassetindexfund.com/ is targeted to institutional investors. The fund of 10 cryptocurrencies screens for security and hacking vulnerabilities, exchange concentration, and ownership concentration by a cryptocurrency's foundation.

25. TRADE CRYPTOCURRENCY CFDS

A contract for difference (CFD) is a trade of a financial asset directly between two parties.

The parties settle the trade directly between themselves. The peer-to-peer blockchain is an ideal platform for facilitating CFD trades. The transaction is secured by encryption and both exchange fees and payment processing fees can be reduced or eliminated.

A CFD trade can provide advantages over trading on an exchange. In the nascent cryptocurrency markets, CFD trades provide the opportunity to find partners to trade illiquid cryptocurrencies. The listing process for new tokens is typically slow. Only a few exchanges may accept a token, and even then, trading volume may be low. Or you may want to use a degree of leverage or short selling not available on the exchanges you use.

How to set it up:
Large institutional traders such as hedge funds often trade CFDs directly among themselves while smaller individual investors typically buy CFDs from a broker.

1. Choose the type of CFD you would like to buy. CFDs are sold on stocks, indexes, currencies and other assets. You will be choosing among different cryptocurrency CFDs. Do you want to trade

PART II. 37 STRATEGIES TO PROFIT IN THE NEW CRYPTO ECONOMY

bitcoin or ether CFDs? Or perhaps you're trading BTC for fiat, such as USD.
2. Specify the amount you're investing and your trading parameters. Are you going long or short? Are you using leverage? How much?
3. A smart contract will be executed at the agreed upon opening price.
4. The contract will be closed at the agreed upon stop loss, take profit, or contract expiry date.
5. The profit or loss will be automatically transferred between your crypto wallet and that of the broker.

26. GAMBLE FOR CRYPTOCURRENCY

Not surprisingly, gambling applications are top money makers in the crypto economy, and not only for the gambling platforms. Gamblers are also making more money on the blockchain, while paying low or no transaction fees. Gambling in cryptocurrency provides many opportunities to take home more winnings.

On the blockchain, gambling is provably fair. You no longer have to worry about an algorithm rigging the game in the house's favor. Since transactions are recorded and traceable, the manipulation of results is impossible. With transparent and verifiable transactions, you no longer have to trust the betting owners to fairly record your wins and losses. You take home higher winnings due to fewer losses to cheating and security breaches.

Even if you're on a losing streak, you can still make money on the digital ledger. On traditional platforms, you finish with your winnings or minus your losses, and fees. When you bet with a gambling token, you become a shareholder on the platform. As a token holder, you share in the profits of the gambling site. Popular games like FarmEOS and vDice are paying players dividends on revenue from gambling fees generated from their thousands of daily users.

Players can gamble anonymously without registering personal data on the platform. If the gambling entity does get hacked, your personal information will not be on it.

How to set it up:
1. Register with a blockchain gambling application. You may be required to provide KYC/AML information.
2. Buy tokens to join the platform. You may be required to purchase the tokens during the ICO or on an exchange.
3. Play your favorite games.
4. Your winnings will be instantly deposited to your crypto wallet.

Tip:
- You no longer have to worry about being restricted from playing. Platforms accepting cryptocurrency circumvent many local laws and payment service regulations that may restrict deposits and withdrawals.

27. GAMING FOR CRYPTOCURRENCY

Virtual currencies are not new to gamers, but taking home larger winnings is. By cutting out high commissions to gaming platforms, low cost peer-to-peer trading on the decentralized blockchain is allowing gamers to earn more. Micropayments with low or no fees allow the monetization of game assets (game skins, virtual cards etc.) and skills. The trading of virtual game assets between players and the bestowing of smaller rewards becomes feasible.

When playing games, the transparent digital ledger provides a fair playing field. Cunning players and manipulative game hosts can always find a way to cheat in games. What if you could play games with zero cheating? Game play is tracked on verifiable smart contracts making it difficult to rig a game. When you trade or sell in-game items, you no longer have to worry about them being stolen. Your war gear, cryptokitties, cards and other virtual assets are traceable on the blockchain. Another cool feature that can help you earn more crypto is the ability to trade game and other virtual assets across game applications. Several gaming DApps have introduced trading across gaming marketplaces. With no large commissions to pay to centralized gaming platforms, more revenues go towards divvying out token rewards to players.

A unique feature of some gaming blockchain applications is the opportunity to become an investor. Game developers can receive support from their peers by way of token investments. As an investor, you receive a share in the developer's future profits. These earnings are in addition to your share of the gaming platform revenue as a token holder.

How to set it up:
Investing in the early stage of a gaming DApp ICO is the best way to buy tokens at a low price. Most tokens will be available on exchanges after the ICO. If you're new to Blockchain gaming, here are a few good places to start.

1. An early paladin in blockchain games, HunterCoin https://huntercoin.org/ cleverly integrates game play with the minting of the HUC coin. Hunters battle for resources and earn coins on a map and transfer them to wallets, all in game play. To incentivize miners to process transactions, miners receive 10 percent of coins banked

by players and 4 percent if the player is killed. The gamification of the blockchain transaction process is a brilliant way to learn how blockchain apps work.

2. By visiting Steem Monsters https://steemmonsters.com/ on Steem and trading cards in Splinterland you can experience the difference of a game developed on an open source platform where everyone shares in the revenues. Steem members earn tokens by investing in, commenting on and upvoting ideas on the Steem Monsters game. Steemian teams of writers, artists and musicians developed the storylines in the 200-page guide. The game co-founders estimate they received value equal to $1 million in development costs from the STEEM community (Source: thecreativecrypto.com).

Many Ethereum games will require you to download MetaMask, which allows you to run an Ethereum node in your browser. Other games may require you to sign up to Steem or another game hosting website.

If you're a developer, you get the digital rights management to the games you develop. Major game developers like Ubisoft are joining the indies and working on developing games on the digital ledger.

28. CREATE A BITCOIN BLOG/NEWS SITE

If your blog is not making money, or worse, you're paying to promote your content, you need to learn how to market on the Blockchain. If traditional blogging has not been an economically productive activity for you, you can put your writer's hat back on. Bloggers are substantially increasing their income through blockchain monetization strategies.

Close to 20 million visitors a month read cointelegraph.com. The Blockchain Blog has 180,000 Facebook fans and 700,000 Twitter followers. Blogs on how to make money and be more productive in work and life are successful, and the Blockchain provides an opportunity to increase your income and improve efficiency in all areas of life. So whether you're providing software engineers tips on how to build better Blockchains or introducing new gaming and travel apps to consumers, demand is high.

How to set it up:
There are many methods to increase the revenue of your cryptocurrency blog, and many pay higher rewards than traditional blog monetization channels.

1. Sign up for Google Adsense and start earning money from ads appearing on your site. Google's ad network is still the main source of revenue for many blogs, but don't overlook the many new opportunities.
2. Many CPM (cost per thousand impressions) marketing networks targeting blockchain apps want you in their network. Affiliate linkers like CoinTraffic https://cointraffic.io/ and Bitraffic https://bitraffic.com/ have hundreds of crypto app users in their advertising networks.
3. Add app affiliate links. Blockchain and cryptocurrency applications use affiliate networks to increase their traffic. Thousands of crypto applications want you in their ad network. Blogging on gambling? BitCasino https://bitcasino.io/ says it will pay you the highest affiliate rewards, up to 25-45 percent, for affiliate referrals who gamble on the site.
4. Blog on Steem https://steemit.com/. Steem rewards tokens to those who blog, comment and upvote content. Bloggers receive 75 percent of the revenue earned by a blog.
5. Blog for bounty rewards posted by Blockchain startups promoting their ICOs and applications. But if you only blog for rewards, you

may lose credibility among your readers. As long as you provide value to readers, you can increase your traffic and earn token rewards on the side.

How to set it up:
- Whatever blog money making opportunities you choose, you no longer have to worry about the spammers, hackers or system downtime that drain money from bloggers on centralized networks. All activity is facilitated by trackable and auditable smart contracts. To ensure transparency, some applications such as BitCasino provide a dashboard updated daily to track affiliate activity.

29. EARN BITCOIN BY GETTING TIPPED

If you want to make money in the Bitcoin world, you can simply ask for a tip. Bitcoin has developed a vibrant and growing tipping culture. There are many ways of receiving a tip in bitcoin. The easiest way is leaving out a virtual tipping jar. "The Bitcoin Jar" has developed a tipping loyalty program. When customers and other visitors visit a company website, they can leave a tip. When the bitcoin jar breaks, customers are rewarded in different ways—one coffee shop gives out free coffees, while an airline hands out free air miles to those who signed up for the tipping jar loyalty program. Many tipping loyalty programs will alert you when their tipping jar breaks via a mobile app.

If you received a tip for each time you helped someone, would you be able to buy a luxury item or a coffee? You can now put a value on how helpful you are at Bitfortip. https://www.bitfortip.com/ In exchange for providing helpful information, those who need help will leave you a tip.

Feeling generous? Bitcoin bots such as TipBit allow you to leave tips for others on Reddit and other social media platforms. The next time

PART II. 37 STRATEGIES TO PROFIT IN THE NEW CRYPTO ECONOMY

you like a post, you can show your gratitude in Bitcoin. Tips are left in micropayments called bits—one bit is equal to *one millionth* of a bitcoin. Most tips are collected by virtual tipping jars (see below). Be creative. Delivering a presentation at a blockchain or other conference? Why not wear a t-shirt with your tipping jar's QR code?

By the way, since we're talking about getting tipped, here's my BTC address and QR code. :)

348H9ntZgXPdS3FFFRAyovvD3vzTFANuLJ

How to set it up:
1. Choose a tipping bot for the social media site you're using.
2. Create an account and link your wallet, if asked. Tips often go directly with the tipping bot wallet.
3. The tipper creates an account, funds the tipping wallet and leaves tips while visiting social media sites.
4. You can then transfer the tips to any wallet of your choosing.

Explore tipping bots for other major cryptocurrencies. Bitcoin Cash users can use Tippr and other bots to get tips on Reddit, Twitter, Telegram and other social media sites.

Many tipping bots are free. Some may add a transaction fee.

30. ACCEPT BITCOINS AS A PAYMENT METHOD FOR YOUR GOODS AND SERVICE

If you're not accepting cryptocurrency payments, you're missing out on over 30 million Bitcoin wallets worldwide, not to mention the wallets of hundreds of other crypto coins, that could be generating you revenue. Doing business in cryptocurrency is one of the easiest ways of earning crypto.

Accepting cryptocurrency can also lower your cost of doing business. BitPay https://bitpay.com/ charges a one percent transaction fee, versus 3 percent or more for fiat payment methods such as credit cards. Eliminating the costs associated with fraud is a strong incentive to move your merchant payments to a Blockchain payment system. Retailer merchant revenues are being eroded by fraud. In 2018, retail merchants were losing $2.94 and mobile commerce merchants $3.29 on every dollar from fraud and related costs (chargeback fees, lost merchandise and revenue), according to LexisNexis® Risk Solutions.

How to set it up:
New e-commerce payment systems are accepting payments in both crypto and fiat currency. Meanwhile, the most popular e-commerce platforms are adding cryptocurrency payment options. If you want to be doing business tomorrow in cryptocurrency, here are some of the platforms to consider:

1. E-commerce giant Shopify has partnered with CoinPayments https://www.coinpayments.net/ to accept payments in over 300 cryptocurrencies.
2. Popular *Coinbase Commerce* integrates with the major legacy e-commerce systems (PrestoShop, Shopify, Magento, and more) and promises to have your cryptojobslist gateway open in minutes.

PART II. 37 STRATEGIES TO PROFIT IN THE NEW CRYPTO ECONOMY

3. BitPay is the leading Bitcoin payment system. The open source platform integrates with 40 payment and point-of-sale systems.

31. RENT OUT YOUR COMPUTER RESOURCES FOR CRYPTO

How would you like to rent out your unused computer hard disk space in the same way you rent out your unused parking space? You could be earning cryptocurrency on the computer storage, cloud storage, or bandwidth you don't use. The distributed blockchain can help you monetize your unused resources by sharing them in exchange for crypto tokens. In the same way cryptocurrency mining uses the shared distributed computing power of many individual computers to mine crypto coins, your unused computer resources can be shared with others.

The concept of shared computing resources is growing in popularity owing to the cost savings. By using open source decentralized storage, the storage provider does not have to pay for storage space. Data storage and communication centers pay top dollar for real estate close to customers to ensure rapid data transmission. Why not rent Tom's unused hard disk space next door? Resources are organized on local nodes. You not only get cheap storage but the data transfer could be much faster. End-to-end data encryption keeps your files and data secure from hackers. Better still, you can rent out your computer resources and get paid.

How to set it up:
More than a dozen blockchain applications are providing shared computing resources, and more are planning to launch. Here are some models to choose from:

1. Storj.io allows you to save and earn on computing resources. As a storage user, you pay only for the storage you use. You can also rent

out your hard drive or bandwidth. The shared computing resources will be available in 2019.
2. Filecoin is a storage marketplace where data centers with unused storage bid for your business. The bidding process ensures competitive pricing.
3. privatix.io is the first peer-to-peer internet bandwidth marketplace. Benefits include faster transmission times by using local bandwidth and a lack of internet censorship on the private network.

32. EVERLIFE–CREATE AN AVATAR THAT EARNS CRYPTO

Being immortal is not a dream.

We have all had days in which we wish we had a body double to complete all the tasks on our To Do list. Have you ever wished you could split in two? Well, now you can. On the EverLife.AI network, you can develop an avatar of yourself. But this is not any dumb clone. The AI-powered network enables you to create an avatar and train it to do tasks. You can actually lighten your workload.

On the Everlife Network, you can do more than duplicate yourself. You can hire avatars to perform tasks for you. Your avatar can also earn EVER tokens by performing tasks for others.

Millions of avatars are connected on the EverLife.AI P2P gossip network. As your avatar performs tasks it gets smarter as it develops skills. Like in any AI network, as data generated across the network is shared, AI functions become smarter. Your avatar can continually increase its knowledge and skills. Best yet, your avatar is not going to get tired like you. Your avatar can work 24/7 in the EverLife virtual world.

How to set it up:
1. Go to EverLife.AI and click on Create Avatar.
2. Find tasks to perform in the EverLife.AI P2P gossip network and get paid in EVER.
3. Use EVER tokens to upgrade the skills and knowledge of your avatar.
4. Increase the price you charge to perform tasks.
5. Use your EVER to pay avatars to perform tasks for you.

33. DEVELOP CRYPTOCURRENCY WIDGETS AND PLUGINS

Widgets put need-to-know information at our fingertips. Widgets and plugins for Windows, MAC, Android, IOS, Wordpress, blockchains and other platforms make our life easier. Those who conduct trade and commerce in cryptocurrency need numerous information tools to operate efficiently in this evolving market.

So your programming skills are rusty or you don't have any at all? There are many programmers for hire on freelance websites with experience in developing mobile apps, widgets and plugins. All you need is a good idea and market demand for your widget.

How to set it up:
First decide which platform you want to develop information tools for. Choose your operating system—Android or IOS, for example. Or perhaps you want to make WordPress plugins for the burgeoning community of blockchain and cryptocurrency bloggers on Medium and Steem. Research popular widgets and find an unfilled niche, or a widget that would benefit from enhancements. Here are some popular information tools:

1. Price tickers and charts. Stock and currency tickers and price charts are among the most popular widgets. Opportunity abounds

for real time price information on major and minor cryptocurrencies and tokens.
2. Currency converters—Coinmarketcap lists 4,000 cryptocurrencies. Billions of conversions across crypto and fiat currencies are conducted daily.
3. Trading tools. Price trends, moving averages, candlesticks—conventional and new trading analysis tools are in high demand.
4. Cryptocurrency payment gateways are popular Wordpress plugins.
5. Donation and tipping wallets are in high demand.

Of course, all of these widgets already exist. But even in the mature Android and IOS app market, innovative ideas can still become overnight blockbusters. Widgets can always be combined and interact in new and useful ways.

34. INVEST IN HIGH YIELDING BONDS, BUT BUYER BEWARE

One lending opportunity is to invest in bonds issued and paying interest in cryptocurrency. Bitbond, for example, is a platform for Bitcoin bonds. An advantage is the higher interest rates paid for loans by smaller companies that cannot access traditional bank lending. The average lending rate on Bitbond is 13 percent. In comparison, if you invest in a corporate bond, the average interest rate in 2018 was around 4 percent. A higher risk of payment default exists but some crypto bond markets will even cover a missed interest rate payment.

How to set it up:
Here are a few platforms offering higher yielding cryptocurrency bonds:

1. BitBond: Receive high interest rates in Bitcoin for lending to small businesses.
2. Solidus Bonds Interest is paid every 30 days in SwiftCoin.

3. TwoGap https://twogap.com/ A crypto bond market with low fees (low Ethereum gas costs)

Bitcoin high yield investment plans (HYIPs) are a way to spike your returns, but beware of scams. HYIPs are being aggressively marketed to cryptocurrency and blockchain investors through social media. These brokers are offering to double your money. It sounds like an attractive investment opportunity.

But always do your due diligence. An HYIP is not a safe investment; it is a Ponzi scheme. An HYIP promises to double your money and for a period you may receive a steady stream of interest payments. The seller of the HYIP is making these payments by selling HYIPs to new investors. When there are no more new investors, the payments stop.

35. SELL YOUR ARTWORK FOR CRYPTO

Whether you're a starving artist or have enjoyed commercial success, selling art in cryptocurrency can open up new markets and help attract new buyers. You may not only attract new buyers of your artwork but also new buyers to the art world. The ability to sell shares in assets is revolutionizing the art market, as well as real estate, diamonds and many other markets. Fractional ownership provides you the opportunity to attract buyers who previously could not afford or justify an investment in your artwork.

The blockchain provides a number of benefits to art buyers and sellers. The low cost of transactions on the blockchain and lack of intermediary makes micro-sales feasible. The risk of trading art is significantly reduced. More than 50 percent of art on the market is estimated to be forgeries and the ownership lineage very difficult to track. Provenance can be tracked on art registered on the digital

PART II. 37 STRATEGIES TO PROFIT IN THE NEW CRYPTO ECONOMY

ledger, which registers an immutable record of each sale. This ownership assurance helps establish and preserve the value of your artwork, which makes it easier to insure and sell.

How to set it up:
Many opportunities exist to sell artwork on the blockchain.

1. Sell your painting in a gallery that sells shares in artwork in cryptocurrencies. Multiple certificates representing a proportional share in one artwork are issued. Popular art dealers on the blockchain include Maecenas and FRESCO
2. Upload your digital art (prints, video, sound) to the R.A.R.E. Gallery https://dapp.rareart.io/
3. List your art at the ATO Gallery, which famously sold Benjamin Katz's painting "Chasing Hearts/Northern Lights" for 150 Bitcoins, the equivalent of $1.25 million USD.

Parisian artist PascalBoyArt https://www.pboy-art.com/ showed real ingenuity by placing a QR barcode on his street art, which collected $1,000 USD.

36. SELL YOUR HANDMADE GOODS/CRAFTS ON ETSY

Your arts and crafts could be earning cryptocurrency on Etsy. Etsy is the online market for handmade goods and unique manufactured items. Etsy allows you to get paid in crypto no matter what your talent—crafting handmade jewelry, making vegan tote bags or designing stickers. Not surprisingly, many crafty sellers are making crypto selling crypto-related goods. Bitcoin gold pendants, t-shirts, slippers, mugs, ties and cufflinks are just some of the items for sale.

PART II. 37 STRATEGIES TO PROFIT IN THE NEW CRYPTO ECONOMY

If you want to HODL more Bitcoin, Etsy buyers love cryptocurrency themes. don't limit yourself to the Etsy market. Also consider other online shops that accept cryptocurrency, such as Shopify and Big Cartel. Many of the major payment shopping carts have added cryptocurrency payment options.

How to set it up:
1. Register for an Etsy or other online handmade goods marketplace account.
2. List your products. Fill out the description form and upload images. Your product images will determine whether visitors click and buy. Refer to one of the many good articles on product photography for tips, such as Etsy's The Ultimate Guide to Product Photography.
3. Go into marketing high gear. Share links to your store and special offers on your social media network. To build an Etsy community, favor other Etsy shops and buy their products.
4. Be sure to include the *Thank you* option after a sale is complete. Send a customized message and offer discounts on future sales and referrals.
5. Share your affiliate links with your social media and Etsy community.

Even better, sell your goods on a blockchain Etsy alternative. It seems only fitting that the handmade goods community should sell among themselves peer-to-peer in a virtual local crafts market without paying high commissions to middlemen. OpenBazaar https://open-bazaar.org/ accepts 50+ cryptocurrencies.

PART II. 37 STRATEGIES TO PROFIT IN THE NEW CRYPTO ECONOMY

37. GIVETRACK IS THE GOFUNDME OF THE CRYPTO WORLD

There are many reasons to accept donations in cryptocurrencies. First and foremost, givers may be more apt to give in crypto for the reasons cited below. Here are a few appeals you could make to encourage donors to open their crypto wallets.

- Put your unused crypto rewards to good use in the world. Almost all cryptocurrency platforms give out rewards. As we do more business on crypto platforms, you will earn more rewards in tokens. These tokens are not play money. Most can be exchanged for major crypto and fiat currencies but like in the traditional economy, most reward points go unused.
- Your donation in cryptocurrency could be worth more. USD is not likely to increase a lot in value but crypto could appreciate considerably. On the other hand, they could also decline substantially in value. The recipient of the crypto donation could exchange most of the currency for a less volatile currency or buy futures and hedge a potential decline in price.
- By donating via the blockchain, we can track and audit your donations and ensure they reach the intended recipients.

How to set it up:
The philanthropic world is opening its hearts and wallets to cryptocurrency. Here are some of the opportunities available:

1. Donate on a cryptocurrency donation site. GiveTrack (https://www.givetrack.org/ only accepts donations in bitcoin.
2. Raise money for your project on a crowdfunding platform for projects with a social good, such as the Root Project https://rootproject.co/pitch-project-new/, Bitgive or Bithope

3. Launch your own crypto philanthropy such as the Clean Water Coin http://www.cleanwatercoin.org/ or the impak Coin https://www.impak.eco/en/europe/
4. Use the giveth.io platform to develop your own Decentralized Altruistic Community (DAC). DACs have raised over $1 million on the platform.

Tip:
- Use a transaction processor and wallet that charges zero fees to nonprofit organizations.

PART II. 37 STRATEGIES TO PROFIT IN THE NEW CRYPTO ECONOMY

BONUS STRATEGIES

I've included four additional strategies for you to consider. These didn't make the cut in the first 37 for either one of two reasons. They're either a little more advanced and require development skills (create a dApp), or they're a bit risky (flash-crash trading), so I wouldn't consider them 'strategies' but more nice-to-haves that depend mostly on luck.

38. CREATE A DAPP

A dApp is a decentralized application built on a blockchain's peer-to-peer network rather than centralized servers. The top DApps by market capitalization are type I blockchains—operating systems, like Android or IOS—on which other dApps run. dApps issue tokens to users to access functions on the app, and these tokens trade as cryptocurrencies on exchanges. Examples by market cap are Ethereum ($21B), Ripple ($18.4B) and EOS ($4.9B). These blockchains are competing on incentives and performance improvements (transaction speed, capacity etc...) to entice you to launch your app on their network.

But what type of app (called a type II DApp) should you develop? Most DApps are built on the Ethereum network, an upgrade of the Bitcoin blockchain adding smart contract functionality—though you should explore other blockchains to see which best meet your app needs. Any functionality can be programmed into a smart contract—processing a transaction, booking a ticket, activating game action. To activate these functions on the Ethereum network, you need to create a token based on the ERC-20 standard.

PART II. 37 STRATEGIES TO PROFIT IN THE NEW CRYPTO ECONOMY

How to set it up:

In this example, we are developing a Type II app—a DApp that runs on an existing blockchain. If you're not a programmer, you will need to hire one. Fortunately, many freelance programmers have experience developing DApps using Java, and Solidity for the smart contract.

1. Create the frontend of the DApp (This is the interface with the Ethereum blockchain).
2. Create a smart contract and program the functionality. For example, a hotel app will provide a booking registration in exchange for tokens while a betting app will generate a random number and reward the winner by depositing tokens in his wallet.
3. Connect the smart contract to the DApp.
4. Deploy the dApp on IPFS—a free hosting service for DApps.
5. Connect your website to the DApp.
6. You will need to install Mask or Mist to run the DApp in your browser.

Fortunately, many DApps have been created to do this work for you. Download the DApp Builder app https://dappbuilder.io/ or a similar DApp to your mobile device or hire a DApp developer. To operationalize the app, you need to distribute tokens to users to activate the smart contract functions.

39. DUMPSTER DIVE FOR COINS TRADING BELOW ICO PRICE

One strategy I've used with success is finding coins that are trading *below* ICO price. Many of them sell-off right after they are listed, so this happens a lot. They almost always spike back up eventually, which makes them good to watch out for. I look at the fundamentals behind coins, the team, and so forth, but I also look for coins that are way below ICO price.

SRN is one example.

- ICO price was 0.47
- Current price is .073 (on October 2nd, 2018)
- All time high was 3.62
- All time low was .068

Most coins have washed out since February 2018 and made full retraces. Buy coins like these that are in the gutter. For projects that are promising, they essentially have precedent to make it back up to their previous highs. On the other hand, many of these coins will die out and be worthless in a year. Dumpster diving is risky so be willing to lose 100% of the money you invest, but certainly favors a shotgun approach.

How to dumpster dive:
1. Go on ICO Drops.com or a similar site that shows the current price of a coin as well as the ICO price https://icodrops.com/ico-stats/
2. Select a handful of coins that are trading below ICO place—you'll find that there are many.
3. The question, then, is whether or not the coin has any future. Conduct a fundamental analysis (product, team, white paper, partnerships, community) to determine whether the project is worth investing in.
4. Many of the large exchanges like Binance and Bittrex won't have smaller cap coins, so you'll have to register on a smaller exchange like Cryptopia or Kucoin.

PART II. 37 STRATEGIES TO PROFIT IN THE NEW CRYPTO ECONOMY

40. ARBITRAGE ON EXCHANGES

Coins on one exchange can be found cheaper on another exchange. You can profit from this price difference by buying low on one exchange, transferring your coins to the exchange with higher prices, and selling your coins at a profit. This is called price arbitrage. Essentially, the arbitrage is a way for a pro-trader to generate revenue from discrepancies between exchange rates.

Arbitrage can be tricky with crypto because it takes time to transfer coins from different exchanges. The time you spend waiting, the coins could drop, defeating the purpose of your arbitrage. Also, liquidity on smaller exchanges can make it harder to sell your coins, and you might get locked into a bad trade, losing money. Try this out using smaller amounts as to avoid this risk. We've found https://arbitrage.coincheckup.com/ to be a good resource to check prices across various exchanges, as well as crypto volume https://cryptolume.co/.

Arbitrage can happen on the country-wide level, too. For example, when the Turkish currency, the lira plummeted, the demand for bitcoin skyrocketed, sending the price of bitcoin up $500 higher on Turkish exchanges. A smart investor could take advantage of this by trading with a contact in Turkey.

How to do it:
1. Setup accounts on various exchanges. You'll probably need to sign up for some sketchy, smaller exchanges all around the world in order to take advantage of arbitrage opportunities.
2. Check one of the above resources to identify opportunities
3. Buy/sell with small amounts of money.
4. Never keep a lot of money on one exchange.

Lastly, you can consider using arbitrage trading bots which will do this for you automatically. Haasbot and Gimmer are two popular options, but you can also hire a freelance developer to build one for you for a cheap.

41. FLASH-CRASH TRADING

A flash crash is a sudden drop in price that is usually a glitch in reaction to aberrations in the market. Usually this is because of heavy selling, or where people automatically start selling large volumes at an incredibly rapid pace to avoid losses.

For example, during one flash crash, ether's price went from $319 to 10 cents on Gdax. After the flash crash, the price bounced back up to the $300 range. Unfortunately, many people's stop loss orders were triggered and they lost enormous amount of money. Other people had buy orders set at various low ranges and were able to buy really cheap ether—they woke up the next day having 10x'd their account. All because of a glitch.

There are flash crashes every once in a while, but there's no way to predict these. The only way to take advantage of this is to set really low buy orders ("stink orders") across a range of coins. Do this if you have some extra money sitting around. But it's rare that you'll get these, and not a strategy you can reliably depend on.

How to set it up:
1. Pick a handful of coins on whatever exchange you're trading on.
2. Set up buy orders at very low prices that would make it worth your investment (there's no intelligent way to do this with technical analysis, and it's rather arbitrary).

3. Set price alerts via your exchange to let you know when your orders execute.
4. Go back to whatever else you were doing.

The large exchanges like Coinbase and Bitfinex are unlikely to have more flash-crashes as they have strong platforms and high liquidity. Consider looking at medium-sized, or lesser-known exchanges. Also, consider the upcoming age of tokenized securities which will require their own set of trading platforms and could provide opportunity for flash-crash trading.

Part III

INVESTING

Chapter 1

THE INVESTOR'S GUIDE TO EVALUATING CRYPTOASSETS

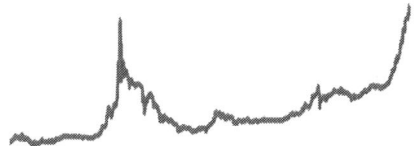

"The single most powerful pattern I have noticed is that successful people find value in unexpected places, and they do this by thinking about business from first principles instead of formulas."
—PETER THIEL, ZERO TO ONE: NOTES ON START UPS, OR HOW TO BUILD THE FUTURE

Most people don't necessarily have the time, technical expertise, or desire to become a trader. Others trade occasionally, but also want to make longer term investments for bigger returns. You may simply have some risk capital that you'd like to put into a high-risk high-reward investment over the long term in the hopes of a 10x–100x multiple over the long run.

Taking the mindset and approach of an investor, rather than as a speculator, is your other option. It requires a lot of effort, research

PART III. INVESTING

and due diligence—not to mention, mental fortitude. You must take a deeper dive into the industry, gathering information and making an investment based on a set of predetermined factors; process is paramount.

In many ways, investing is a lot easier than trading. Since your decisions are not driven by daily market movements, it's less stressful and emotionally jarring, and thus less susceptible to short-termism; by definition you're looking at months or years down the line before cashing out. Because cryptocurrency is a new investment asset class in a new and rapidly changing industry, it is lacking in real valuation frameworks (you can't look at the 20-year history of the company because it just started). There are many parallels to venture capital and angel investment.

Practically speaking, investing in crypto comes in a couple of flavors.

1. Buying a coin during an ICO, STO or crowd sale at a discounted price.
2. Buying any token that you deem undervalued and holding it for the long term.

For the sake of simplicity, I haven't included angel investing in the traditional sense of the word (money for equity). That said, if you meet the minimum net worth requirements of an accredited investor, you can get access to a range of private deals that most people can't through platforms like *Coinlist*. Many of the investment principles below still apply regardless of the amount you're putting in.

CHAPTER 1. THE INVESTOR'S GUIDE TO EVALUATING CRYPTOASSETS

WHY IT'S IMPOSSIBLE TO ASSESS A CRYPTO PROJECT

The big thing to bear in mind when approaching the valuation of crypto projects is that nobody really has a solid understanding of this space yet—it's like traveling back to 1994 and forecasting that, in 2018, Apple would be the first company to be worth $1T. That's the 1994 GDP of the United Kingdom! There is no equivalent to a George Soros or Warren Buffet with proven track records for crypto. The closest we have are moonshot thinkers and venture capitalists like Tim Draper who are making a big bet on the future.

It's all being figured out and debated by the token-economists.[35] The valuation methods in the market are evolving, too. The proof-of-stake (PoS) coins have tangible market caps but can't be compared to proof-of-work (PoW) coin values secured through mining—so it's all still a work in progress as amateurs, as well has hedge funds and venture capitalists on the institutional side, try to find value bets. In reality, no valuation models are viable yet as we don't have a baseline to measure across the asset class.

This doesn't mean that analysis is useless, but it should be conducted with the caveat that things could change quickly. It's also important to stay up to date on new analysis and valuation techniques and be ready to discard your previous assumptions. With that said, I'll share my valuation technique, which takes a multi-faceted approach, and will do my best to keep it updated as our understanding changes.

---

35 Chris Burniske does a great job providing an in-depth technical analysis of crypto projects in his book *Cryptoassets*. Michael J. Casey and Willy Woo's analysis are also worth checking out (they post regularly on Medium).

MARKET CAP AND 100X RETURNS

Market capitalization traditionally represents the size of a company. In crypto, *market cap = circulating supply x market price*. You can go to Coinmarketcap or any listing of cryptocurrencies to find this value.

The market cap for Metaverse (ETP), as of this writing, would be calculated as 54,191,917 ETP x $0.688237 = $37,296,867. It's ranked #83 by market cap on Coinmarketcap, bitcoin being the coin with the largest market cap.

How does 100x happen?

A coin that has a low market cap has more room for growth. When the price of Bitcoin jumped from 10k to almost 20k in a period of less than a month, you could have doubled your money in that very short period. However, if you had invested in a project like Ripple at the start of 2017 (.034 cents) and held it for just one year (shot up to $3.50), you would have made a 10,200% gain! Just $1,000 would have turned into $100,000.

Generally speaking, though, coins with lower market caps are more risky to invest in because they are less liquid. Selling them on an exchange is harder because many people aren't trading them. But as we saw with Ripple, they provide opportunity for ridiculous returns. While many traders spend time making a few hundred or thousand bucks here and there, you truly only need to identify one or two projects like Ripple to make life-changing amounts of money.

CHAPTER 1. THE INVESTOR'S GUIDE TO EVALUATING CRYPTOASSETS

As you do your own research, keep in mind the risk versus reward trade off as outlined in the graph above. The top 50 or 100 coins by market cap are probably not going to be the next moonshot coins that make you a gazillion dollars. Of course, I could be wrong, and crypto has a way of completely destroying any previous expectations. But generally speaking, coins that have private funding, a strong team, a working product and strong community, as well as a low market cap, are the ones that can grow 100x in price over a 2-3 year period. So, how do you identify the potential moonshots?

THE MOSAIC APPROACH TO CRYPTO INVESTING

Mosaic theory involves collecting information from different sources, public and private, to calculate the value of a security. Applying the mosaic theory is as much art as it is science. An analyst gleans as many pieces of information as possible, determines if they tell a story that makes sense, and decides whether to recommend a trade[36].

The Team and Culture

A strong founding team is critical to the success of any business. In tech, generally people look for at least one technical founder and a co-founder with expertise in the industry they're tackling. Without technical expertise and strong developers executing the business plan, it is practically hopeless. The easiest way to learn about the founding team is to look at their LinkedIn profiles. Ask the following questions:

1. Is there at least one technical founder?
2. Do the founders have a track record of success?

---

36 "Mosaic Theory," *Investopedia*, https://www.investopedia.com/terms/m/mosaictheory.asp.

PART III. INVESTING

3. Do the founders have experience in their vertical?

It's okay if the team doesn't have experience in blockchain. Many do not considering how new the industry is. As one blockchain entrepreneur said, "One year working in the blockchain sector full time is the same as four years' experience in more traditional sectors." More importantly, do they know about their vertical? For example, if a founder is launching a startup to disrupt the supply chain network in coffee, do they have experience in either the coffee or supply chain world? If not, they better have a cofounder who does (an advisor is not enough).

You'll often see "advisors"—sometimes dozens—listed on the team section of a project's website. This can be deceptive and falsely paint the picture that the company is impressive in size and has a lot of credibility. Anybody can be an advisor, and any company can list an advisor, so generally I take it with a grain of salt. However, it is worth noting when the advisors *are* competent. This requires you to do some digging.

For example, at first glance John McAfee is a prominent investor and advisor to blockchain startups, and although he has a well-known name, his track record is questionable. McAfee invented the McAfee Antivirus software years ago (a notable achievement) and has since been jumping from country to country running from the police under suspicion of murder and tax evasion— not to mention his less than serious antics on Twitter. Compare him to someone like Naval Ravikant, who is the founder of Angellist and Coinlist, and has a slew of successful investments including Twitter and Uber. A simple 10-minute search for both McAfee and Ravikant online will give you a pretty good idea of the vast difference in their professional reputations and business successes.

Second, look at what employees are saying about working there. Is the CEO described as focused and driven, or does he never meet his deadlines and is rarely in the office? Is the work environment productive, healthy? I recommend checking Glassdoor to get opinions and reports from people working there. You can set up Google Alerts for that company name to see what news is being reported about them on a daily basis.

Of course you can make the argument that many entrepreneurs who didn't have any industry experience have been successful—Mark Zuckerberg being an obvious example. However, Zuckerberg had amongst other things a tight-knit market (Harvard students) where he could test his product, and was later able to learn from the mistakes of MySpace and Friendster. Keep in mind that the Mosaic approach takes several factors into account, which is the beauty of it. The "science" is the measurement of your criteria, but *how you weigh the importance* of some factors in relation to others is the "art" of it.

One further piece of advice from author and entrepreneur Tim Ferriss: *"Have the founders ever had crappy service jobs, like waiting tables or bussing at restaurants? If so, they tend to stay grounded for longer. Less entitlement and megalomania usually means better decisions and better drinking company, as this stuff normally takes quite a few years."*

Partnerships
The value of hidden partnership potential is often overlooked. The addition of one partner can drive significant revenue growth and lend credibility to a company. This cred is particularly important for

PART III. INVESTING

blockchain startups trying to get their feet off the ground. One way to build credibility is for employees to leverage their networks and connections to establish partnerships. A good example is the Lightyear acquisition of Chain that formed Interstellar. Chain was notorious for having Citi, NASDAQ and American Express as clients of its Sequence product.

Adam Ludwin is the founder of Chain, and has since moved on to become the CEO of Interstellar. Tom Jessop became head of Chain after Adam left, after one year. Then, in 2017, Tom left Chain and moved to Fidelity where he now heads their Crypto asset division, which received a lot of press for announcing a custody solution and other potential offerings in 2019. Connecting the dots from NASDAQ to Chain to Stellar to Fidelity reveals some potential underlying value not realized yet and a decent chance some of those partnerships/relationships will create long-term competitive advantage and market gains—in this case for Stellar as the investment.[37]

Community Engagement

All crypto projects have their own Telegram and Discord groups where they engage with their users, developers and investors. These are typically open to the public and you should be able to gain access pretty easily. Activity and engagement can be deceptive—just because there are lots of "users" or "followers" on social media or Telegram doesn't necessarily say much. The startup could have spent a lot on marketing and paid for people to join through, for example, Telegram boosting

---

[37] You can connect these dots by digging deep into people's LinkedIn and Crunchbase profiles, which commonly list where they have worked. For Adam Ludwig's example, see: https://www.crunchbase.com/person/adam-ludwin#section-partner-investments.

CHAPTER 1. THE INVESTOR'S GUIDE TO EVALUATING CRYPTOASSETS

services that allow you to buy followers.³⁸ Rather than measuring the number of users, look at the depth and quality of conversations and interactions. Are the employees/founders keeping people updated? Are they answering questions people have? Or is the group full of spammy messages and zero added value?

I also like to check if the company has a Medium page or an active blog somewhere. While not everyone is going to be posting daily, it's important to hear the voices of the founder and employees, and their vision for their product/market. In particular I'm fond of long-form blog posts, detailed technical explanations and use-cases of a particular product, as it shows the company is really thinking and sharing their ideas.

Community engagement also encompasses the resources they're investing into building the community via partnerships. For example, Slovakia based smart-contract platform Decent (DCT)³⁹ hosted two separate hackathons in Europe where they brought together developers to build on top of their platform. They awarded prizes to the top winners. I thought this was a great example of community investment and engagement, as the ROI on events is hard to measure but usually beneficial over the long run.

Another example is the training program launched by French blockchain startup Tezos, which raised over $200m USD in one of the largest ICOs to-date. They had some political disagreements internally but have since bounced back, full-force, committing to train 1,000

---

38 This service tracks group growth over 24 hours and tries to pinpoint how much is related to airdrops/bounties, which can help determine how much non-airdrop/bounty group growth spiking is related to bots and spam: https://icoholder.com/en/deep-statistic/telegram.
39 Decent, https://decent.ch/about-dct/.

developers to use the Tezos platform.⁴⁰ This is a good example of strong community engagement and demonstrates a longer-term view.

The White Paper

Many white papers are copy-pastes of the Ethereum white paper. Those are obviously scams. The challenge is that most are generally not peer-reviewed, full of technical jargon, and a pain in the butt to read. For that reason I would take white papers with a grain of salt, just like I wouldn't focus 100% on a pitch deck for any startup, but rather look holistically at their team, market size, product, ability to execute, and so on. The idea, though, has to be at least half-decent. One important question to ask is *why does this have to be on the blockchain rather than just a database?* If you have a hard time answering this question, search online to see if the company has already answered it, or reach out to them directly.

> *"If you just take a database and shove some hashes in it, that does not an immutable blockchain make! But it does make some good money for consultants."*
> —ANDREAS ANTONOPOULOS

Traditional Funding

When a VC firm like a16z or big-name investor backs a company with a cash injection, it's worth noting. Anyone can go and issue a coin, but when accredited, institutional and non-token fundraising comes into play you can take that as a signal that these investors have done some of the due diligence for you. Security token platform TrustToken⁴¹, for instance, raised $20m USD from Andreesen Horowitz in 2017. You

---

40 "Tezos to Fund and Train 1000 Developers," *Tezos Foundation*, https://tezos.foundation/news/tezos-foundation-commits-funding-to-train-developers.
41 TrustToken, https://www.trusttoken.com/.

can check funding rounds on websites like Crunchbase. https://www.crunchbase.com/

The Product

Crypto is unprecedented in the investment space in that there's is a lot of money floating around (from ICOs) but no great incentives to get actual work done. Many of the projects have a small team with a few developers and have suddenly raised a lot of money. However, there's little to no actual governance since regulations are still being framed. There are no deadlines from investors, no real repercussions and no real shareholder action that can be taken for mismanagement since tokens are not equity and don't grant any rights to a company's earnings or performance (buying a crypto token is not like buying a share of a company). In fact, most of them don't even have a working product. Compare this to your average startup that has done a Series A and has a CEO and investors pushing them to meet project deadlines.

Product may be one of the most challenging areas to assess due to the novelty of the industry but one of the most important. Are they seriously working on their products and is there any real progress? Are they meeting their deadlines? I recommend getting your hands dirty here and checking Github to see the progress of their projects. Youtubers like Datadash and Ivanontech, amongst others, regularly offer Github reviews of individual crypto projects as well as tutorials. You don't have to be a programmer to do this, but it helps (you could try befriending one).

Reddit and other AMAs are a great resource where in communities like Kin "investors" get to fling questions directly at the CEO who will try to clear up misconceptions, provide answers regarding the

PART III. INVESTING

product/roadmap and use what little power they do have to keep the team honest and accountable.

Another method (referred to in classic investment terms as "scuttle-buttting") is to talk to the company directly to gather info. It makes sense to get first-source information straight from the horse's mouth, as it might be quite different than what you read online.

Liquidity

The worst case scenario is not being able to cash out because you cannot sell your coins when you need to—particularly when the price has multiplied and you have achieved your price target. How important this is will depend on your risk capital, time horizon and personal investment style. Microcap coins that are not listed on any big exchanges and offer almost no liquidity can be risky bets, even if you have a long-term horizon. One solution is to simply stick with mid-to-large cap coins, or those that trade on at least a couple of well-known high volume exchanges.

There are also instances when projects are *delisted* from exchanges because they fail to meet criteria for trading volume, so regardless of your time horizon it's beneficial to keep track of a coin's performance: usually a delisting is bad news for the project and indicates some deeper issues. If you can't find liquidity on a crypto exchange, you can also consider looking at bitcoin/crypto dealers who facilitate international trades.

Market Cap

The traditional calculation for *market cap = circulating supply x market price*. Taking a look at *Coinmarketcap* today, I can see bitcoin's price is $5,260 x circulating supply of 17,383,150 BTC = a market cap of

$96,666,837,347 USD. Theory suggests that the larger the market cap, the slower the growth rate. [42]

This metric can be useful in building a balanced portfolio, gauging upside and assessing risk. For example, if I look at the fifth largest market cap coin right now and think it's a great buy, I have to ask myself what I think the upside is. Could it go 5x, or 10x? That would mean it'd surpass bitcoin's market cap—do I think that's likely (maybe not)? A large cap coin like Ethereum may be slower moving, but more "stable." A lower or mid cap coin might have more room for growth or volatility, but it also might be riskier.

But hold on a second. The assumption when calculating market cap is that tokens are like stocks, which is a *big* assumption. In fact, there are several problems with this comparison. First, tokens don't come with any shareholder rights or any claim to future cash flows. Second, the supply of stock issuance is fixed, whereas the supply of tokens isn't fixed, and new coins continue to be issued over a period of months/years. These emissions of new coins are going to be scheduled differently, so it's hard to compare the market cap between the two accurately—there could be a big difference.[43] Lastly, lots of illiquid coins and "lost tokens" are included in estimates of circulating supply that don't necessarily accurately reflect the reality.

Is there a better way to gauge market cap in crypto? Crypto entrepreneur and blogger Nathaniel Whittemore has a few suggestions, although many are experimental at this stage. "Realized Capital"

---

[42] XRP and XLM were exceptions to the rule but generally, yes, the more established the more slow moving.
[43] Nathaniel Whittemore and Clay Collins, "The Problem With Market Cap," *Nomics Blog*, https://blog.nomics.com/essays/crypto-market-cap-review-emerging-alternatives/.

factors in the coins that have not been claimed or have been lost. BCH, for instance, had a market cap of $60b USD, but adjusted for Realized Cap was more like $11b USD (which would rank it quite a bit lower!). To explore more assessment methods, check out the Honeybadger presentation and links in the footnotes. One final tip is to simply rely less on market cap and look at trading volume and liquidity; if the coin is not listed on exchanges and no one is trading it, dock it major points.

THE SCUTTLEBUTT METHOD

The scuttlebutt method uses firsthand knowledge from discussions with employees, competitors and industry experts to make conclusions about an investment. Employing both the Mosaic Theory and scuttlebutt method together involves gathering small pieces of non-material information and combining them to form a material conclusion. In other words, you're reaching out and talking to people.

I've found that most people in crypto are pretty friendly and open to conversation. Everyone is eager to connect, share their ideas and also receive feedback. In fact, the industry thrives on this sort of positivity. This makes the scuttlebutt method easy to use. Those who have time on their hands and are seriously committed could actually take a trip to the company's office—obviously easier if they're nearby. But you can conduct a lot of this research online, via chat and Skype, and have conversations with founders and developers. You'd be surprised how easy it is to get a hold of people. I contacted 30 blockchain CEOs on LinkedIn and almost all of them responded.

Outside of the company, you can also reach out to the following people:

- Customers

CHAPTER 1. THE INVESTOR'S GUIDE TO EVALUATING CRYPTOASSETS

- Suppliers/vendors
- Competitors
- Analysts who are following the company (check Bravenewcoin, Cointelegraph, Forbes, Youtube, Nytimes, etc.)

Check the following sites to reach out to people in the companies:

- Github
- Medium
- LinkedIn (get a premium account to access a wider network and send paid messages)
- Quora
- Instagram
- Facebook
- Glassdoor
- Reddit
- Steem.io
- Angellist https://angel.co/
- Telegram

The questions you ask founders and employees are going to depend on what you're looking for. Perhaps it's just one piece of information about their product or hiring plan. Or maybe you're really trying to understand their business but need help wrapping your head around it (that might be a red flag in itself). In any case, here is a list of questions you can consider asking:

- What are the company goals for this year?
- What is your long-term goal?
- What's your biggest challenge?
- What actions are being taken to overcome said challenges?
- How will X affect your company? (stablecoins, regulations, etc.)

- How many people are you hiring now?
- How will your plans change if the bull/bear scenario switches?
- Do you have enough treasury to sustain a 2-year slide and consolidation?
- What concrete timeline do you have for a product launch/update or roadmap for the next 2 quarters?
- How many developers do you have?

Make the Decision and Follow Your F*cking Rules

Your decision is as good as your research. Once you have concluded your research above, you're ready to pull the trigger. Evaluating crypto assets is still a new game and nobody has got it all figured out; in fact, it's so new that Google Docs keeps underlining the word "crypto assets" thinking I made a typo. I hope one day it's in the dictionary. If you're not feeling confident, ask yourself why, and do more research—talk to more people if necessary, ask yourself *What's the worst that could happen?* and make sure you're covering your downside. Go in less heavy and reduce your risk. But when you're ready, pull the trigger. Don't deviate.

THREE TIPS TO REMEMBER

The first step is to find your edge. What industry do you know about? What informational asymmetry do you have? Do you know a lot about the supply chain industry, or real estate, or do you think that finance is the future of blockchain? Maybe it's healthcare. If you're confident that you know more about X industry than most people, use it. Find that edge. Don't veer outside of these lines; most failures come about when people forget what they're good at and break their own rules.

Second, establish your process, conduct research and identify these opportunities. There has to be a framework that you follow. While there might be outlying reasons outside of the process that influence an investment decision, these can often lead to trouble. It's best to list a set of criteria and then apply them to all the projects you're considering. For example, the screens could consist of team, product, community engagement, current price, industry and exchanges the project is listed on. You should use the same factors in every assessment you make; otherwise, you're not being objective or consistent and will invariably miss something.

Third, use "no" as your default answer—assume you will not invest in most projects. Weed out the bad apples. Rely on your process and strict framework for identifying what you think could be successful within your area of expertise; ignore your investment plan at your own peril.

Chapter 2

MY PROCESS IN ACTION: WHY I INVESTED $11,250 IN 0X (ZRX)

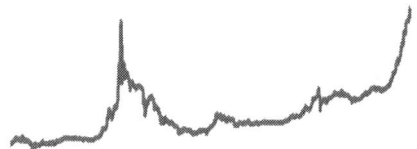

Let's take a look at what makes 0x attractive as a potential investment—and why I invested several thousand $USD in the project. Keep in mind that when evaluating a crypto project as a potential investment, the key metrics—from the growth rate to how value is created in a network—differ from those of mainstream investments. Here are 5 key metrics I use.

WHAT IS 0X (THE ZRX TOKEN)?

"0x is an open protocol that is designed to offer a decentralized exchange as part of the Ethereum blockchain. 0x is made using a protocol that involves Ethereum smart contracts that allow those around the world to run a decentralized exchange. The team behind 0x strongly believes that in the future, you will find thousands of tokens from Ethereum and that 0x can provide an efficient and trustworthy way to exchange them. 0x is designed to be different from

> *both centralized and decentralized exchanges, providing the best possible combination of features."*
> —HTTPS://0XPROJECT.COM/

1. THE MAFIA EFFECT

You can have a mediocre product and a great team and do well, but a great product and a mediocre team is a hopeless endeavor. Blockchain is tricky because it's such a new industry. There are no real "experts" in the same way that there are pros in computer science, neuroscience or any other established field that's been around for at least a couple of decades. This makes assessing the team in a blockchain project a challenge.

Look for Startup Experience

That said, it's possible to identify transferable skills. If the founders of a project have successfully started and exited companies in the past, or have been part of a startup team, this gives me some reassurance that they know how to handle a fast-paced, chaotic startup environment. On the other hand, if the founders have only worked for Microsoft or Apple and suddenly decided to ride the blockchain wave, jumping into a startup with zero startup experience, I would be more cautious. I'd check whether they have good external advisors or other employees with startup experience.

The early players in any vertical in any industry can have a sort of "Mafia effect." Most famously we had the Paypal Mafia, whereby several employees from Paypal left and started their own ventures that ended up becoming ultra successful. Former Paypal employees include Elon Musk (SpaceX, Tesla), Peter Thiel (Palantir), Reid Hoffman (founder of LinkedIn), Steve Chen (cofounder of Youtube), Yishan Wong (CEO of Reddit), and quite a few more. Ripple/R3 are

CHAPTER 2. MY PROCESS IN ACTION: WHY I INVESTED $11,250 IN 0X (ZRX)

their own mafia—Ripple managed to recruit Ben Lawsky, a former NY regulator responsible for creating the infamous BitLicense, onto their board. Talk about an inside edge!

Give Extra Points for Crypto Space Bench Strength

Coinbase could be sort of a Paypal Mafia of the crypto world. Perhaps, it's still too early to tell. At the very least, many companies have external advisors from Coinbase, and a few employees have left Coinbase to join new ventures. The 0x (ZRX) project was one that stood out for this reason. Three of the co-founders of 0x were previously at Coinbase.

While Coinbase is a centralized exchange and doesn't exactly live up to the libertarian ideals of a decentralized marketplace, it provides necessary market liquidity and is a key player in getting bitcoin trading to the masses. It's also the largest crypto exchange in the U.S, has $225 million in funding, is based in Silicon Valley, and was #1 in downloads on the iTunes App Store for quite some time. They are doing something right. So when employees from Coinbase leave to start a company or join another business, it's worth raising your eyebrow.

What is most intriguing to me is the nature of the 0x business—it's a decentralized exchange, which is exactly the opposite of Coinbase. Why did these three people from Coinbase leave and join 0x? Perhaps it's a disagreement about ideologies (centralized vs. decentralized), or perhaps they know something we don't and have a hunch about the future of blockchain. Regardless of the reasons, the benefits of

PART III. INVESTING

having ex-Coinbase members on your team are numerous—chiefly, the know-how they bring from a crypto startup team.

Being in the know in Silicon Valley and one of the first cryptocurrency exchanges in the US is huge. There's also the potential that, if 0x is on good terms with Coinbase, maybe the ZRX coin gets listed on Coinbase. And what do you know—as of me writing this, it has been announced that the coin is being listed on Coinbase Pro (which will almost certainly create more liquidity and an increase in price).[44] Other members of the team include engineers from Google, Facebook and Apple who have worked on digital products. While they are not blockchain projects, again, they bring tech expertise in a fast-moving industry.

2. METCALFE'S LAW/NETWORK EFFECTS

Metcalfe's Law states that as the number of nodes in a network increase, the value of that network increases. One telephone is useless, but when you have two you can communicate. When you have 100, then things get really interesting. This applies to blockchain projects. And your product doesn't even have to look pretty, it just has to work well (amongst other factors). Craigslist didn't have the best website, but it had the most users for a classified site. eBay had a pretty basic website too, but it had a first-mover advantage, captured many users and was able to dominate its market.

Hundreds of coins are ERC-20 based coins, meaning they are built on top of the Ethereum Blockchain. Blockchain startups choose ERC-20

---

44 The likelihood of an increase in price is becoming less sure particularly in a bear market, but in theory it should be a growth catalyst as it has been in the past. When the market becomes bullish, I see it likely that coins on large, liquid exchanges like Coinbase popping off.

CHAPTER 2. MY PROCESS IN ACTION: WHY I INVESTED $11,250 IN 0X (ZRX)

tokens because they run on the most reliable smart contract platform, which is led by a great dev team. As the number of projects increase, the value and necessity of Ethereum to the smart contract ecosystem has increased with it. This explains the several-thousand percentage price increase in ether between 2017 and 2018. Many blockchain projects have the potential to do the same. Any project that captures a certain vertical—say online gaming, could move on to become the dominant token or platform used by gamers. Of course just because it can doesn't mean that it will. A lot of other factors have to be just right, like timing, the team, the tech, and of course a bit of luck.

Assess Traffic Flow Growth

The 0x project, a decentralized open source protocol, plans to light up network nodes by solving a lot of the problems associated with decentralized exchanges. It's technically not an exchange, but can be used by anyone to create a decentralized exchange. The transaction fees are practically zero. Unquestionably, demand will be huge for decentralized exchanges in the coming years. Since the average consumer is still wrapping their heads around Bitcoin, they will flock to Coinbase or Bittrex to buy bitcoins and do little else. As crypto investing goes mainstream, a protocol like 0x will be the backbone for many of these decentralized exchanges, and that's a good spot to be in.

Following Metcalfe's Law, the value of the 0x protocol is quite low at this point in time since there are few nodes in the network—that is, not many companies or people using it. Even if it is traded as a coin on Coinbase, what is the actual utility beyond speculation? The true value won't be realized until there are actual applications and projects (and many are already being built). But once that happens, 0x has, in my opinion, the potential to add significant value to the ecosystem. From this perspective it's not a good short-term investment, but a mid-to-longer term one. And because it's longer term I'm willing to accept drawdowns on my investment of 30-40%.

3. PRICE PSYCHOLOGY

Follow Your Own Research, Not the Herd

How the market currently thinks about a certain technology can obviously impact its price. Market psychology is largely about the media, and social media has taken us to a new level of information dissemination. Even individual investors like the eccentric John McAfee (there's a great documentary about him on Netflix) can shill a coin on Twitter, causing massive fluctuations in price. This is herd mentality at its finest. During the big hype cycle in late 2017, early 2018, we saw many cryptocurrencies pop off the charts, making unreasonable gains with wild valuations.

Many friends asked me how to buy bitcoin and when they should sell. I can't make those decisions for anyone but myself. This was risky territory and I always tried to dissuade them from putting up any amount that they wouldn't be willing to lose. One comment I got frequently that scared me was ,"I don't want to buy bitcoin because it costs so much." More disconcertingly, many people didn't understand the very basic technology. Nor did they understand that they could lower their risk by purchasing a few satoshis (1 Satoshi = 0.00000001 BTC), that all these currencies are divisible. You don't have to buy one bitcoin, you can buy any fraction that suits your current situation and goals.

Beware of Media Hype and the Ripple Effect

Fortunately, or unfortunately, this is how a market is created; people in the know vs. people not in the know. This is how money is made. That and a bit of luck. Now, another interesting example comes from

CHAPTER 2. MY PROCESS IN ACTION: WHY I INVESTED $11,250 IN 0X (ZRX)

Ripple (XRP), whose price multiplied more than 4x over the span of a couple of weeks in late 2017 and early 2018. This resulted in the coin topping the charts in the top five cryptocurrencies. It stood at around $1 for one XRP for several days. Looking at the chart at this time, Bitcoin was hovering over $10,000, Ethereum over $1,000, and Litecoin in the several hundred dollars.

Many investors who didn't understand even the basics of how market capitalization works saw Ripple as "cheap." It only costs $1! CNBC picked up on this and started talking about how to buy Ripple. When major media starts instructing the average consumer how to buy, you know you've reached the top of the market and should be very cautious. It came crashing down pretty quick, and then CNBC ran another special on "how to sell Ripple."

While I expect people have learned from their mistakes, I don't think we've reached market saturation or mass consumer adoption. Plenty of newcomers will start using cryptocurrencies in the next few months and years. Even day traders and professional traders are not immune to these psychological traps & tendencies. The 0x protocol has the ZRX token, which has hovered between #40-80 in total market cap in the latter part of 2018, fluctuating between 60c and $1. When we think about market cycles in terms of bull and bear, I like to ask myself, "Which coins will people flock to in the next bull cycle?" Surely the ones that get media attention, but also the ones that seem 'cheap' and have nice round, emotional numbers. I think 0x falls into that category (under $1 and hasn't had a big 10-20x market pump).

4. OPPORTUNITY COST OF OTHER INVESTMENTS

Whenever we make a decision to focus on a particular investment, we forego other options. Investing in 0x, for example, means that I can't use that money elsewhere. It means that I should be fairly confident and have good reasons for choosing this one and not another. Of course, you can choose several investments depending on your appetite for risk, the amount of risk capital you're willing to invest, and how you choose to split your portfolio.

When I first started trading cryptocurrencies I took the popular "shotgun" approach and bought several coins in the hopes that one or two would make disproportionately large gains. I was just starting out and didn't know what I was doing, so figured this was a good strategy.

During a bull market, it almost doesn't matter what you choose. The majority of altcoins made very large gains in 2017, and if you had randomly selected to invest in any of the top 30 projects on Coinmarketcap, you would have done very well. That said, many of the coins also fizzled out. Many of the projects and ICOs were scams and retraced to 90% of their price within a year. That means you could've also lost most of your money if you didn't withdraw/cash out in time.

Find an Information Edge

At this point, most people would advise you to diversify. There are many reasons people diversify their investments, but it's primarily to avoid having all of your eggs in one basket and getting wiped out. I also think it's because people don't know what they're doing. Those are Warren Buffett's words, not mine.

Most people don't spend hours and hours researching, nor are they actively involved in the industry they are investing in. They diversify because they don't know how to make more informed choices. But if my friend the hydroponic farmer tells me about his investment in a new hydroponic tomato company, I am going to listen. There is informational asymmetry—he knows something about the industry that

CHAPTER 2. MY PROCESS IN ACTION: WHY I INVESTED $11,250 IN 0X (ZRX)

most people probably don't—and that's valuable. So when evaluating why ZRX might be in a good position to do well, compare it to other projects and, remember, the most valuable information is expert information.

Seek High Growth Crypto

Many large blockchain projects have already been through several boom and bust cycles. They've ICO'd, 10x'd their prices, dropped back down to the ICO price, went back up, and then tapered off at current prices. It's certainly possible that some of those coins will continue to gain in value, but it's unlikely that they will increase 10x or 100x in price again in the next bull cycle. At least in the world of cryptocurrencies, the newer projects that haven't had their "time to shine" tend to take off and gain traction.

In other words, there's more upside potential for newer projects than some of the older projects that have already seen incredible price increases. While Bitcoin can be a "stable" investment, do you think it's likely to pop off and make a 20x or 30x gain in a month vs. a project that hasn't had a single bull cycle? I think not. I believe ZRX is an interesting coin for this reason because it has significant traction in the market, support on major exchanges, great tech, a great team, and the many other reasons I've stated above, but it hasn't seen the ridiculous gains that we've experienced with other coins. It has room for growth.

5. LONG-TERM SURVIVABILITY

There are generally two types of projects to choose from, coins or tokens. The majority of tokens are ERC-20 compliant and based on the Ethereum blockchain. Yet many tokens don't fair so well because, while they use Ethereum's tech, they are very centralized around their own figureheads (projects that aren't open source and centralized could easily fall apart if the lead developer or founder suddenly left). Many haven't delivered on any significant projects, while others have completely dissolved, the recent case of Cofound.it (CFI) being a good example. The crowdfunding platform for blockchain startups was basing its service around ICOs, which are dying out. As ICOs began to be crowded out of the market by a new form of crowdfunding (see Security Tokens), the founders shut the business down and redistributed all the coins.

Invest in Coins With Strong Network Effects

Even if a few developers leave, Ethereum will likely continue to thrive. Like Windows OS, it has established itself as a platform that so many others depend on, yet different from Windows, the Ethereum Blockchain hosts ecosystems with powerful network effects amplified across platforms by cross-compatible ERC-20 tokens. Ethereum won't die even if Vitalik does (that's a big IF, as it's possible he's an extraterrestrial sent to save the human race). It makes sense to accumulate coins that have their own ecosystem, at least as one measure. Decent (DCH) is one example, as is Tezos (XTZ), and of course ZRX. 0x is an open source protocol that allows DApp ecosystems to interoperate. As long as there is traction in the early stages, use cases and strong community support, then it's less likely to be shut down even if some of the core members leave.

Avoid Obscure Exchanges

One final related point—there will always be risk of low liquidity when you're trading low market cap coins. It's largely unavoidable, but as long as the coin is listed on at least one big exchange, your risk can be significantly reduced. There are other newer projects with great teams that I'm also interested in investing in, but they're riskier because they're not liquid or on obscure exchanges. Even if they do make a

CHAPTER 2. MY PROCESS IN ACTION: WHY I INVESTED $11,250 IN 0X (ZRX)

10x gain, or worse, if they lose 50% of their value, what happens if I can't sell? Personally, I'm not going to put 10k USD into one, high risk coin that I won't even be able sell in the case of an emergency. ZRX is listed on major exchanges including Bitfinex and Coinbase (which is a good sign) and has yet to see a big price increase like many other projects. I think for this reason it's undervalued and makes for a very interesting project.

ROGUE DEVELOPERS AND FURTHER COMMENTARY

There are several shortcomings to using Metcalfe's Law and no method is perfect. On the blockchain, volume will flow to second layer solutions and sidechains making volume calculation harder to accomplish and Metcalfe's Law less accurate.

Like any investment, there are certain considerations to keep in mind and it's important to keep an eye on the project in case there is a good reason for me to divest. So, what would trigger me pulling out of 0x?

At the time of writing this, there was a hard fork in the 0x protocol, whereby a few developers from a big decentralized exchange built on top of the 0x protocol decided to rewrite the code and go their separate ways. At a first glance, you might conclude that the future of 0x is uncertain. Forks can happen very naturally and are an important part of progress in the ecosystem, so this could actually be a good thing, but from an investor's perspective it is a red flag as the fork could render the current 0x token worthless.

Upon digging deeper, though, we find evidence of a struggling DEX (decentralized exchange) going rogue in a bear market over a couple of disagreements, and their decision to fork coming from a position of seeming desperation rather than choosing to double down with their current resources. The "exodus" only involved a couple of developers from one decentralized exchange.

Ultimately I don't see any cause for alarm. What would give me pause is if we saw several of the core developers start to leave and work on other projects, with nobody picking up the slack. If the Github repository was dead for months and no new projects were being built on top of 0x, I would reassess the business and decide whether or not to pull out or stay in the game.

Chapter 3

17 TIMES PEOPLE WERE TOTALLY WRONG ABOUT THE FUTURE

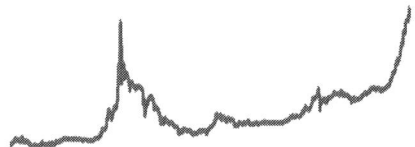

"Google's not a real company. It's a house of cards," said former Microsoft CEO Steve Ballmer. Today, Google's market cap is $100 billion more than Microsoft's.[45]

"Neither RedBox nor Netflix are even on the radar screen in terms of competition," Blockbuster CEO Jim Keyes told the Motley Fool in 2008. "It's more Wal-Mart and Apple." Blockbuster filed for bankruptcy in 2010. Today Netflix is worth $61.93 billion.[46]

---

45 MG Siegler, "Google Loses Engineering Director Who Once Caused Steve Ballmer To Melt Down," *TechCrunch*,
https://techcrunch.com/2009/07/13/google-loses-engineering-director-who-once-caused-steve-ballmer-to-melt-down/.
46 Graham Rapier, "13 Quotes From Bosses Who Mocked Technology and Got It (Very) Wrong," *Inc*, https://www.inc.com/business-insider/boss-doesnt-understand-technology-mocks-trend-wrong.html.

PART III. INVESTING

David Neeleman, the CEO of Jetblue Airways, invented electronic ticketing for airlines two decades ago. "When I proposed the idea, people laughed at me, saying no one would go to the airport without a paper ticket."[47]

"The horse is here to stay, but the automobile is only a novelty—a fad." This was advice from a president of the Michigan Savings Bank to Henry Ford's lawyer Horace Rackham.

"What can be more palpably absurd than the prospect held out of locomotives traveling twice as fast as stagecoaches?"—*The Quarterly Review*, March, 1825.

"There is not the slightest indication that nuclear energy will ever be obtainable. It would mean that the atom would have to be shattered at will."—Albert Einstein, 1932.

"There is no reason for any individual to have a computer in his home."—*Ken Olson, President, Chairman and Founder of Digital Equipment Corporation (DEC), in a talk given to a 1977 World Future Society meeting in Boston*

"I predict the Internet will soon go spectacularly supernova and in 1996 catastrophically collapse."—Robert Metcalfe, founder of 3Com, inventor of Ethernet.

"Children just aren't interested in Witches and Wizards anymore."—*Anonymous publishing executive writing to JK Rowling, 1996.*

---

47 Edward Hallowell, "Overloaded Circuits: Why Smart People Underperform," *HBR*, https://hbr.org/2005/01/overloaded-circuits-why-smart-people-underperform.

CHAPTER 3. 17 TIMES PEOPLE WERE TOTALLY WRONG ABOUT THE FUTURE

"We are not interested in science fiction which deals with negative utopias. They don't sell."—*A rejection letter from a publisher writing to Stephen King.*

"We don't like their sound, and guitar music is on the way out."—Decca Recording Company on declining to sign the Beatles, 1962.

With over fifteen types of foreign cars already on sale here, the Japanese auto industry isn't likely to carve out a big share of the market for itself.—*Businessweek*, August 2, 1968.[48]

"'Is the world going to come to an end?' I say, 'I don't know.' I don't know whether this will be a bump in the road—that's the most optimistic assessment of what we've got, a fairly serious bump in the road—or whether this will, in fact, trigger a major worldwide recession with absolutely devastating economic consequences..."—*Senator Robert F. Bennett, Chair of the Senate Special Committee talking about the dangers of upcoming Y2K.*

"If excessive smoking actually plays a role in the production of lung cancer, it seems to be a minor one."—*W.C. Heuper of the National Cancer Institute in 1954.*

"Stocks have reached what looks like a permanently high plateau."—Irving Fisher, economics professor at Yale University. This was in 1929, just before the Great Depression.

"Before man reaches the moon, your mail will be delivered within hours from New York to Australia by guided missiles. We stand on

---

48 "Bloomberg BusinessWeek," *Wikipedia*, https://en.wikipedia.org/wiki/Bloomberg_Businessweek.

the threshold of rocket mail."—*Arthur Summerfield, U.S. Postmaster General.*

"Everything that can be invented has been invented."—*Attributed to Charles H. Duell, Commissioner, U.S. Office of Patents, 1899.*

WARREN BUFFET VS. TIM DRAPER

Share volume and price spiked in insurer Travelers (TRV)—not coincidentally, the day the media revealed that Warren Buffett's Berkshire Hathaway had increased its stake. The famous value investor moves markets, so if Warren Buffet does not like a stock or sector, does it matter?

It's no secret that Warren is baffled by bitcoin. He does not even consider it an investment. Should we crypto enthusiasts be worried?

The Oracle of Omaha, one of the most successful billionaire investors of all time, was also nonplussed by technology stocks. He's a value investor. Value investing is an investment strategy in which stocks are selected that trade for less than their intrinsic values.

Buffet doesn't invest in new technology companies because they do not meet his value investment criteria. He buys undervalued stocks when they're at an all time low, and then holds the stock forever.

He first invested in Apple in 2016, not 20 years ago. That's pretty recent. But now Apple has had decades to prove itself as an established company, and meets his high criteria for investment.

Buffet spends hours each day reading annual stockholder reports. He's looking at companies with healthy free cash flows, a specific

CHAPTER 3. 17 TIMES PEOPLE WERE TOTALLY WRONG ABOUT THE FUTURE

P/E ratio, favorable profit margins, a growing net worth/shareholder value, and a reasonable return on shareholder equity (ROE).

The wealthy value investor invests in products he uses and companies like Coca-Cola and McDonalds that have been around for a long time. This has worked out pretty well for him.

His motto is **"just show me the cash-owner earnings."**

Tim Draper is a long-time tech investor, venture capitalist and crypto-bull. He was the first person to attach catchy messages and links when Hotmail first came out. He basically invented viral marketing. Draper was also an early investor in Tesla and SpaceX.

Draper bought 32,000 bitcoins in 2014 for an undisclosed price (the BTC that was seized by the government from the dark web market, Silk Road). It's estimated that he's got around half a billion dollars in crypto, but maybe more.

Draper's bitcoin investment has realized a 25x ROI in just three years. The venture capitalist also put $100m USD in Coinbase, the largest crypto exchange. Coinbase has more active accounts than Charles Schwab does and is valued at $8 billion USD.

> *"It's better to be the one encouraging the changing of our own industry than to be the one who gets surprised by it."*
> —TIM DRAPER

There's no way that Buffet would have bought that much BTC—a technology (hell, not even a company) that was less than five years old.

It'd never happen, simply because Draper and Buffet have very different investment styles dating back to the very start.

The financial tools and valuation frameworks in crypto and publicly listed companies are, at least for now, worlds apart. Startup companies are betting on an idea. They might have a working product and revenue but they're so new that you can't use many of the same metrics that Buffet uses to analyze them.

Buffet has probably cringed at the mania in the crypto space, which is the antithesis to his investment philosophy and to be avoided at all costs. He's not a speculator and he doesn't *trade* stocks. He doesn't drive a Purple Lambo with butterfly doors...the billionaire drives a 2006 Cadillac XTS, a $45,000 car.

Berkshire Hathaway would be verbally destroyed by shareholders if 9 out of 10 companies in its portfolio were performing poorly for more than a few years. Draper, being a VC on the other hand, expects most of his investments to have small gains, and one or two outliers to provide a 10x, 20x, or 100x ROI.

But in some ways, the two investors aren't so different.
Buffet has famously promised to never sell a share of American Express, Coca-Cola or Wells Fargo. Draper has shown similar bullishness and faith in buying and holding Bitcoin—"it's the future of commerce."

Both investors stick to their guns and focus on their area of expertise. But, hey, it's worked out pretty well for these billionaires.

Buffet hasn't commented much on blockchain tech, but he has denounced bitcoin as one big bubble. I think he's kind of been forced

CHAPTER 3. 17 TIMES PEOPLE WERE TOTALLY WRONG ABOUT THE FUTURE

to make a statement on it. In interviews he's admitted that he's not a tech investor, and it's not his area of expertise.

Mind you, he's been wrong before, like when he invested in IBM...

He also didn't invest in Amazon or Google, which he regrets not doing. Buffett admits, "I was too dumb to realize."

Who's right?
While Buffet is certainly one of the greatest investors of all time, he lacks the track record of successful investments in the space, along with the technical expertise.

Simply put, domain expertise is critical. We're probably better off looking at investors with a track record in tech—like Tim Draper, Naval Ravikant, Marc Andreessen, Peter Thiel and Chris Sacca.

This isn't to say that Buffet won't eventually invest in a blockchain-based company. If he decides to make any sort of bet on a tech company in the future, there's at least some likelihood that the company will have a product or service offering related to crypto (i.e., an investment in Facebook would mean he's indirectly supporting Whatsapp's development of a stablecoin).

For now, Buffet's largely skeptical and negative comments on bitcoin say little about crypto or the blockchain industry as a whole. There are people more qualified than him to make that call, and smart people have certainly been wrong about the future!

Chapter 4

NEVER GIVE UP YOUR RAILROADS

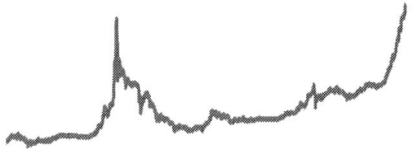

"Monopoly is the condition of every successful business."
—PETER THIEL, ZERO TO ONE

I rolled doubles and moved my pewter terrier eight spaces, landing on a green property, Pennsylvania Avenue. The property costs $320 and statistically is one of the least landed on and most expensive in the game (a much worse deal than the dark blues because you need three greens before you can start building houses). I had another one of the green properties, so this would be my second one.

The problem was, I had just gone on a buying spree of all the light oranges and had started to build houses on those three beautiful properties. They weren't cash cows—yet. Once the players went around the board a few times—a matter of time and a bit of luck—I knew that statistically other players were likely to land on them. In other words, I was in a good spot, and I just had to wait. Patience.

I looked down at the $173 I had in my hands. I couldn't afford this green property unless I mortgaged a couple of my other properties.

PART III. INVESTING

Someone once told me that you should always buy properties when you landed on them. *GOD DAMMIT.*

I think I got bad advice. There are always exceptions to rules. Buying this green property, from everything I could gather, was *not* a good idea. I'd be strapped for cash and I could get wiped out. Nobody else would get a monopoly because I already had the other green, so I already had an advantage and could prevent others from building houses. I didn't need this other green to win the game. Too risky.

But I still couldn't shake the feeling that I 'should' buy it, perhaps because it was accepted as common knowledge that you should do so. There's an aspect of human psychology at play, a feeling that you're missing out on an opportunity—"What if this happens?" or "What if that happens?". Though I am a daydreamer, I realized that being lost in blissful imaginings would be an unnatural response to giving up on an opportunity. It's hard to feel *joy* when contemplating the lost opportunity cost—at least at first.

I was obsessed with Monopoly. I still have several editions of the game—Euro monopoly that's all in French, National Parks monopoly (Yosemite is Park Place) and NFL monopoly, even though I never watch football. When I was in university I would organize 'Monopoly Night' on Friday nights. I would make popcorn and order beer and pizza. Instead of going to class, I would practice playing monopoly online and plan my moves. The first time I held Monopoly Night two people showed up and we had a four-hour game and got drunk. I thought it was a lot of fun. After that first game, nobody ever came to Monopoly Night again (except for me).

I started playing Monopoly again recently and realized how relevant it is to trading and investing. Maybe the countless hours spent playing during my childhood somehow influenced my perception of risk and reward in the world.

YOU CAN'T HAVE ALL OF THE PROPERTIES.

You simply cannot own it all. There are other players in the game. When you get all the properties of a color group you can start building houses on top of that, which will bring in more rent. You need a monopoly first. This takes time; you have to go around the board a few times to get them. Sometimes you need to trade properties with others in order to gain a monopoly. Other times you need to make sacrifices like mortgage other properties so you can afford to not miss out on a big deal (although I don't recommend going to these lengths in real life!).

A losing strategy is to buy one property from each color group and never have a monopoly. By not building an empire, you will never spread yourself thin but nor will you ever specialize deep enough to reap any meaningful rewards. Actually, that's not entirely true. If you *really* made this your strategy and did everything you could to get one color from each player, it might make for a really weird and drawn-out game. And while nobody would go bankrupt they might all quit from boredom; but you would prevail. It's so crazy it just might work.

I have criticized the "shotgun" approach in crypto—buying lots and lots of microcaps in the hopes that one will gain significant value. The problem isn't that it doesn't work, it's that many people could make a lot more if they did a bit of research. What if you're REALLY right about three companies, or one, and put a good chunk of capital into that?

First, start with a vision of timing and how things will play out in the market to curate your more granular choices—what's more likely to see growth first—payments and tokenized securities or travel and insurance? I'm not 100% certain, but there seem to be a lot more wallets and payment startups entering the crypto space than travel and insurance, so this is one indicator to consider. Have different buckets for different time horizons and verticals. Buffet famously said, "Diversification is protection against ignorance. It makes little sense if you know what you're doing."

Have a Monopoly of knowledge and assets in a certain area. What are all of the insurance- or gaming- or travel-focused blockchain companies? Start there and go deep, using sources like Angellist, LinkedIn and Crunchbase to list companies in the space. Build up your "houses" on those properties, and forego the others when it's tempting.

WRITE DOWN YOUR STRATEGY AND MEMORIZE IT.

I bought a book called the *Monopoly Companion* years ago that drastically improved my Monopoly skills. You could call it a self-help book, as it helped me take my game to the next level. There are people out there who decry the successes of others as largely luck-based and discredit 'self help.' There is definitely a lot of fluff out there; empty promises with little justification. There's also a lot of common sense, well-structured ideas and practical processes that you can follow. Look for the latter.

Mr. Monopoly's tip sheet measures the *payback, cost, frequency and power* of each property. That is, how much $ can you make from each

CHAPTER 4. NEVER GIVE UP YOUR RAILROADS

property, how much it costs, how frequently people land on said property, and what the final "power score" is—a combination of the previous three factors. This is super useful for its simplicity but also for its focus on a digestible number of factors.

Here's how it translates to crypto:

Trade for monopolies that can dominate quickly. What do you have that is of value to others? How can you accumulate wealth without taking big risks? A simple example is asking to be paid in bitcoin (or whatever currency you prefer), whether you're a business or individual. There are dozens of ways to accumulate cryptocurrencies without necessarily trading them. You will make the most money by gaining an edge, not trying to compete with institutional investors and algorithms (it's a losing battle). Find your niche.

Don't overextend yourself and deplete cash too early. You can't play the game if you run out of cash. I cringe when people put 99% of their assets into digital tokens—it means they have lower protection against risks, and it also means they have less ammunition to buy new investments or take new trades. This is particularly useful advice if you're too trigger happy; sometimes sitting on cash for a while (like, during a bear market) is the best strategy.

Never give up your railroads. The railroads are not the most profitable Monopoly properties, but they are consistent cash flow generating ones (especially if you have all four of them). Don't give up the day-job that generates cash flows to trade, invest or start up a company full time. The founders of massive online glasses retailer Warby Parker were all in school or working as they built up the business in parallel;

only once it was profitable and they knew they were onto something did they eventually dedicate themselves to it full time.[49]

Pay attention. An important rule in Monopoly is that when someone lands on your property you have to notice it and ask for your rent. You have to ask for money or else you get none. You also have to pay attention and be laser focused—where are the opportunities that others don't see? Are you exposing yourself to more risk than you need to? What's the worst-case scenario?

Forget the rules. I really hate using terms like FOMO or Hodl or *When Moon?* Having a common language is important, I get it, but I think it implies that they are somehow new concepts. They're not. People have been FOMO'ing and trying to Moon forever. They've been impatiently waiting for their treasure chests and their exits and their lucky streaks. We just have different words for it nowadays.

---

49 Kimberly Weisul, "How Warby Parker Took the Risk Out of Its Business," *Inc*, https://www.inc.com/kimberly-weisul/how-warby-parker-took-the-risk-out-of-its-business.html.

Chapter 5

11 INVESTMENT TIPS TO REMEMBER

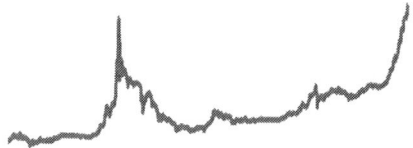

*"If you let your learning lead to knowledge, you become a fool.
If you let your learning lead to action, you become wealthy."*
—JIM ROHN

1. BE AWARE OF YOUR ACTUAL RETURNS

Fast forward to the future and consider the true value of your investment over time. While this requires an extra step, it will save you from shooting yourself in the foot with false assumptions about cryptocurrency gains. As always, taxes should be considered as part of your investment strategy, but taxes on cryptocurrencies may be treated differently. First, consider your total net return after taxes. Capital gains tax varies by country, and there are often higher tax rates for short-term capital gains; that is, if you sell within one year of buying.

PART III. INVESTING

Crypto doesn't always fall into capital gains, though, so check the tax law specific to your country.

Second, in the stock market investors take inflation into consideration and the true value of the dollar over time. In crypto, the more pertinent analysis would be your real return compared to bitcoin's or ethereum's price during that same timeframe. For example, if you bought X coin (selling your bitcoin or eth to make the purchase) and X coin went up 5x in a 6-month period, you might be happy with your return. However, if ethereum's price went up 8-fold in the same period, then you would have been better off holding your investment in ethereum. This goes back to the idea of market cap dominance, which we discussed earlier.

2. BE A CONTRARIAN

> *"A classic definition of a "shrewd investor" was "one who bought in a bear market when everyone else was selling, and sold out in a bull market when everyone else was buying."*
> —THE INTELLIGENT INVESTOR

Paypal founder Peter Thiel prefers not to look at the "trend," as trends tend to die a quick death. "I prefer a sense of a unique mission to solve something that other people are not solving," Thiel says. The best investors are contrarians. They are patient and often wait years to reap the rewards of their investments. They are not hasty in their decision making. They see what others fail to see and are happy to pull the trigger when everyone thinks they're wrong. They spend countless hours researching, asking the tough questions, and understanding their industry better than anyone else. It can be difficult to go against the crowd, but that's where the best investments are usually made.

CHAPTER 5. 11 INVESTMENT TIPS TO REMEMBER

We all know the age-old adage of "buy low, sell high," but in reality most people do the opposite. Being contrarian can simply be doing the opposite of what others do. If you buy what everyone else is buying, chances are that it's already over-bought. Buying the hype and selling the news has proven fruitful so far.

Investor Benjamin Graham (author of the *Intelligent Investor*) advises, "Buy when most people including experts are overly pessimistic, and sell when they are actively optimistic." Detractors, skeptics and even friends will often persuade you that you're making the wrong decision. Be careful about who you tell what, and whose advice you follow—do these people have a track record of success or are they overly pessimistic? Hedge fund billionaire and risk-analyst Nassim Taleb says that, "When you're judged by reality, it's a completely different dynamic than when you're judged by your peers."

3. BE FLEXIBLE AND ADAPTABLE

The right investment depends on your penchant for risk, your area of interest and expertise, timing and a host of other factors. Mining bitcoin was profitable in the early days but the barriers to entry are higher and more expensive now. There are dozens of other token options, as we've explored, that are still in the early stages of price discovery and technological development worth researching. Bitcoin may have the strongest brand on a consumer level, while other currencies are more anonymous (and thus have that small factor advantage I like).

Contrary to how VC and PE works with capital lockup periods, crypto offers 24/7 liquidity, so you can risk adjust over time. This allows you to be adaptable. Making an investment decision is not a one shot motion—ongoing due diligence to validate your hypotheses and ensure that there are no holes in your thinking over time is still

PART III. INVESTING

necessary. If something smells off, it could be a good time to reevaluate and exit the investment. You can risk adjust over time and confirm expectations in stages instead of waiting for a big press release to find out something publicly that could have been figured out earlier.

Other times it's better to do nothing, and not act too hastily because it feels like a lot is going on; jumping into something with this mindset is bound to disappoint. John Templeton, pinned the 'Christopher Columbus of investors,' says that, "There are times to sit on cash, because sometimes cash enables you to take advantage of investment opportunities." [50]

4. YOU *WILL* MISS SOME DEALS

Billionaire investor and super angel Chris Sacca regrets more the investments he passed on than those that "failed."[51] For example, Chris had an opportunity to invest in the early team of DropBox, but he wrongly compared it to Google Drive and thought Google would crush it. He even stayed in an Airbnb before it went mainstream but when he had a similar investment opportunity, he felt that the accommodations posed high risk. "I felt someone would get murdered or raped there," Chris said. Of course, that's probably true; with scale, the sheer number of people using Airbnb (or any other large consumer service) is bound to result in some crimes. The risk of harm distracted him from the potential of the investment.

---

50 Nikki Ross, "Lessons from the Legends of Wall Street," Chicago: Dearborn, p. 188.
51 Alex Konrad, "How Super Angel Chris Sacca Made Billions, Burned Bridges and Crafted the Best Seed Portfolio Ever," *Forbes*, https://www.forbes.com/sites/alexkonrad/2015/03/25/how-venture-cowboy-chris-sacca-made-billions/#38ff45846597.

Over 2000 ongoing cryptocurrency projects are listed on Coinmarketcap, and many more are on the way. It's impossible to sit down and analyze all of them, let alone talk to their founders if you decide to invest a larger chunk of money. When you decide on one investment, there's always an opportunity cost because you're choosing to say "No" to others. There will inevitably come a time when you come across an investment, decide it's not worth your money, and then later find out it's gone on to become the next Airbnb, Dropbox or Facebook. In those cases, it's going to sting.

Chris noticed that there was one thing in common in all of his failed decisions/missed calls—the negative case dominated the analysis of whether he should invest or not. The solution, then, is to do a post-mortem on your decision making. The best you can do is learn from your mistakes and ask yourself the question, "Did you make the wrong decision or the right decision based on your process?" If your process was good, then you just had bad luck; if you find there was something faulty in your process, correct it immediately and move on.

This ongoing process of analysis, reflection and correction should apply to existing investments (since crypto affords that possibility) as well as exited/closed investments. It's process based and shouldn't be deviated from based on whims. Whatever part of it can be automated (Google alerts, scheduled meetups with founders/teams for updates, AMAs, etc..) should be in order to minimize time spent and maximize signals.

As Ray Dalio says, "Pain plus reflection equals progress."

5. MEDITATE

Countless studies show meditation's effectiveness in increasing focus, reducing anger and anxiety, and improving overall well-being. It also allows you to quiet that little voice in your head. Neuroscientists have identified the part of the brain (it actually consists of several parts) that's active when you're not focused on anything or doing anything in particular—the default mode network ("DMN"). There's still a lot of research to be done, but studies have shown that the quieting of the DMN is linked to creativity, but overactivity in this area is associated with anxiety and depression. Brain scans on advanced meditators[52] have shown a significant quieting of their DMN region. Lessened activity in the DMN allows you to experience the present moment with greater objectivity, less clouded by your feelings.

Even just two weeks of meditation, for 10 minutes a day, can start to produce noticeable effects. Sharon Salzberg, cofounder of the Insight Meditation Society, says that, "Mindfulness is the basis for insight." She recommends 20 minutes of meditation per day. For those who are intimidated by the number of options and Silicon Valley takeover of all things new-age-ish, meditation is quite straightforward and can be practiced simply with breath focus. No need for the apps, classes, seminars and consumerist crap typically peddled as necessities to the masses. Check out a book called *The Miracle of Mindfulness: An Introduction to the Practice of Meditation* by Thich Nhat Hanh. One of the first chapters focuses on the sensation of breath going in and out of the nostril—that alone can change your life!

---

52 Annie Wilson, "Meditation and the Default Mode Network," *Inner Light*, https://www.inner-light-in.com/2015/03/default-mode-network-meditation/.

6. BE A LIFELONG LEARNER

Navil Ravikant is a crypto investor and CEO/co-founder of AngelList, a platform for startup investing. His advice for students and life-long learners: "IQ can be traded for Emotional Intelligence—if you're really smart you can figure out your emotions."

We're bound to be wrong sometimes but can often go a long time without realizing it, either out of fear, ego-driven decision making or a lack of general self-awareness. "If you're just curious as to how things work and are more concerned with figuring it out correctly than being right, then you put yourself in a very powerful position," Ravikant advises.

Three simple methods to increase emotional intelligence:

1. **Journal every morning:** By writing, you can become more accountable to yourself. In the morning our minds are teaming with worries, hopes and dreams. By putting your thoughts down on paper, you can get all those angels and demons out of your system so that you can move on with the rest of your day and focus on the important stuff. Or, maybe, through this form of contemplation, wherein you let your feelings and thoughts flow freely through you, you come to realize that you've been running away from a challenging task that needs to be addressed. I also ask myself questions like "Who can I help today?" and "How can I get out of my comfort zone?" Framing objectives in question format in an

open-ended fashion allows you to dissect your issues and goals into actionable steps.

2. **Schedule a weekly self-performance review:** Years ago I started the "weekly review" whereby I would set a recurring event on Sunday nights. Every Sunday I sat down for a 30-minute meeting with myself when I would review my values and goals for the quarter, a list I keep in Evernote. I would have a list of responsibilities at work. I'd run through this list and make sure that I was doing these things, or had set aside time to do these things for the week. Create and customize your own review, including everything from your current portfolio needed to make progress on your goals. Creating a simple checklist and setting a recurring reminder on Google calendar has worked the best for me.

3. **Be specific about how you feel.** "Emotional granularity" is your ability to differentiate between very specific emotions. A child might say they are "happy" or "sad," but as we get older we can better identify our feelings with greater precision. Instead of just happy, it's "I'm feeling energized, relieved and a little bit mischievous—like it's five o'clock on a Friday." In other words, rather than feeling an emotion as one solid block, you understand how to sift through the granules of each emotion. New research suggests that people with higher emotional granularity are better able to cope with difficult situations.

The biggest step to developing this skill is to use more specific words and concepts to describe your emotions. The next time you feel an emotion creeping up, spend time defining it and write it down—don't fall into the trap of just saying "good, bad, pleasant or unpleasant." To get started, start exploring different emotions via the list in the footnotes.⁵³

7. EXECUTE FAST, BUT DON'T RUSH

Mike Jones, former CEO of MySpace and founder of startup studio Science, recounts the story of a missed opportunity from pivoting too slowly. He invested in a pre-prepped meal kit startup called *Freshdish*, and management decided to switch from a subscription-based to a non-subscription model. This was before subscription businesses really took off, so it wasn't so obvious that this was a bad call. Around this time successful startups (competitors) like *Blueapron* were on the rise. When they realized that their subscription model was the right way to go after all, it was too late and *Blueapron* already had a dominant market share.

Investigate before you invest. After doing your homework give yourself a few days to breathe, get second opinions and come back to the decision. Of course, don't wait too long as speed can be vital. It's certainly possible to lose out on opportunities, but more money has been lost from acting in haste than it has to careful planning. You could pull the trigger without thinking and win $1,000 but the lesson you would have learned from thinking slow and waiting could have won you $100,000 over time in other situations... the whole give a man a fish, feed him for a day thing.

---

53 A list of emotions: https://web.sonoma.edu/users/s/swijtink/teaching/philosophy_101/paper1/listemotions.htm, and 100 more: https://www.vocabulary.com/lists/535865.

8. IF YOU MAKE (OR LOSE) MONEY, TAKE A STEP BACK

When people make money they often get caught up in the excitement; the gamblers mindset might push them to "reinvest" that money in something risky to further increase their returns. Others may feel that since they suddenly have come across money they deserve a new lifestyle. This is not sustainable. If you just made a gazillion dollars, don't rush to reinvest all that money. Author and investor James Altucher gives this piece of advice: *Don't change your lifestyle for at least one year.*

> *It requires a great deal of boldness and a great deal of caution to make a great fortune; and when you have got it, it requires ten times as much wit to keep it.*
> —NATHAN MAYER ROTHSCHILD

9. PROTECT YOURSELF FROM BLACK SWANS

Everything is fine until it's not. Nassim Taleb defines a Black Swan event as an event that comes as a surprise, has a major effect, and is often inappropriately rationalized after the fact with the benefit of hindsight. The computer, WWI, the 2008 financial crisis, 9/11, and Brexit are all examples of Black Swan events. They're not all necessarily negative (as in the case of certain inventions), but it depends on which side of the table you're on. The danger is best exemplified in Taleb's description of the "turkey problem."

CHAPTER 5. 11 INVESTMENT TIPS TO REMEMBER

"Consider a turkey that is fed every day. Every single feeding will firm up the bird's belief that it is the general rule of life to be fed every day by friendly members of the human race 'looking out for its best interests,' as a politician would say. On the afternoon of the Wednesday before Thanksgiving, something unexpected will happen to the turkey. It will incur a revision of belief."

Taleb's advice is to avoid becoming the turkey by identifying areas of weakness and turning them into advantages; or at least making sure you're not 100% wiped out. Use the barbell strategy: invest 80-85% of your risk capital conservatively and a small percentage in highly speculative, but potentially high return, cryptocurrencies, startups, etc. There's a chance these high risk investments will go to zero (at least 3/5ths of startups fail), so you want to be investing money you can afford to lose.

Earlier I mentioned that diversification is for those who don't know what they're doing. This holds true, but the barbell strategy here is relevant in terms of *managing risk*. Taleb applies it to investing in ETFs and index funds, which might be right for some people but not for others.[54]

More importantly, have emergency funds and an overall financial plan. Play only with what you're okay losing and then take the discretionary funds and put them into well-researched, planned out and high conviction ideas, like some of the crypto projects we've discussed.

---

54 With the impending corp/fed debt problems from the US/EU and Japan, index funds and passive equity-based investments may not turn out to be the safehaven beta-catching asset classes we always thought they would be. For more, see "The Coming Economic Debt Bomb" https://www.thestreet.com/investing/stocks/beware-of-the-coming-economic-debt-bomb-14584620.

10. CHALLENGE YOUR ASSUMPTIONS

Franz Reichelt was a French parachute inventor who lived over a 100 years ago. One day he decided that he would demonstrate his great new invention by jumping off the Eiffel Tower in Paris. His good friend was also an inventor and had created parachutes that *actually* worked. Looking at Reichelt's parachute he warned against it. *"Reichelt, you fool. The surface area of your material is way too small!"* Reichelt didn't listen.

At that time, most inventors used dummy models to test their parachutes. Reichelt was so sure that it would work that he insisted on jumping himself. He spent months petitioning the French police to allow him to jump. On the day of the jump, spectators tried to dissuade him. Friends pleaded. The police tried to stop him. He eventually snuck past security, ignoring them all. Reichelt jumped, his parachute immediately tangled, and he plummeted to his death. The next day the newspapers reported on the reckless inventor, cementing his name in history as *"The Flying Tailor."* The moral of the story: Being 'certain' and not testing your assumptions could get you killed. Don't let your ego drive your decisions.

> *"When you're surrounded by people who share the same set of assumptions as you, you start to think that's reality."*
> **—EMILY LEVIN**

CHAPTER 5. 11 INVESTMENT TIPS TO REMEMBER

11. SURROUND YOURSELF WITH THE RIGHT PEOPLE

The half-life of content is becoming increasingly shorter—that is, the accuracy of facts is decaying faster and faster.[55] It's becoming harder to keep up with the most relevant content as well as to find high quality content. Beyond the information overload, it's just simply hard to focus. One day this problem will be solved, perhaps by flipping the incentives of the online advertisement model. That's what Brendan Eich, the creator of Javascript, is trying to do with his blockchain startup Brave (BAT). For now, the solution to nurturing high quality content has been to create a paywall for users to join. Whose advice would you trust more? 1) Random trolls on Reddit, or 2) Long-form content created by a closed community of serious investors/traders with a proven track record. Bad advice is usually given for free.

You should ultimately make your own investment decisions and not just follow others. Shadowing a mentor can be very useful until you're confident enough to trade or invest on your own. Becoming an accredited investor will allow you to gain access to exclusive crypto projects on Coinlist, but this is out of reach for most people considering the minimum net worth requirements. Another solution is to go to high quality meetups, or join a paid community. Surround yourself with people smarter than yourself. It is worth the investment and can eventually have a much greater pay-off, both knowledge-wise and by paying dividends many times over.

---

55 "Half Life: The Decay of Knowledge and What to Do About It," *Farnham Street Blog*, https://fs.blog/2018/03/half-life/.

Chapter 6

TOKENIZING THE WORLD

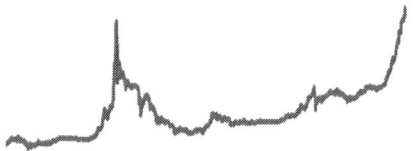

Consider this: only one-third of the world's wealth is held in cash[56]. The rest is held in securities (stocks, COD's etc.), real estate and other assets. You can't always easily *sell* those securities—you may own your house but you can't simply get $400,000 for it in cash tomorrow. A lot of wealth is locked up. But what if you could convert the value of an asset into digital tokens that could be traded and recorded on the blockchain?

Currently, millions (billions, maybe) of dollars worth of art is sitting in museums around the world. The museum owns the art, or some rich benefactor is allowing the museum to exhibit the painting. All that capital is locked up on their walls.

Here's an idea: if you're a museum, you could keep the right to exhibit the work of art, but sell off the right to the capital appreciation of the

---

56 Jeff Desjardins, "All of the World's Money and Markets in One Visualization," *The Money Project*, http://money.visualcapitalist.com/worlds-money-markets-one-visualization-2017/.

piece in the form of User Issued Assets (UIA's). So, you're disaggregating the 1) rights to exhibit, and 2) appreciation. The museum could keep the right to exhibit it 90 percent of the time, and then assign exhibition rights for 10 percent of the time to the top two shareholders of the UIA.

A physical asset in the real world is represented by tokens in the digital world. Large buyers would come in and buy these tokens, in hopes that the tokens would appreciate over time. Perhaps these tokens could be listed on an exchange (or maybe only open to private investors), creating liquidity in the market.

Tokenization makes it possible for anyone to own a piece of an artwork. Fracturization allows tokens to be divided into even very small units and sold to individual investors. In other words, you could go see the Mona Lisa and own part of it, too.

TOKENIZED SECURITIES

For an investor, tokenization provides the prospect of virtually entering the auction at Sotheby's to buy a share of a painting or luxury real estate (perhaps the size of a very small LEGO block) in London's Belgravia district or Tokyo's Minato Ward. What is the best way to invest in tokens and get your own piece of a Warhol or townhouse in Manhattan? A new crowdfunding vehicle called the security token offering (STO) is making it easier to issue and sell tokens with the extraordinary ability to comply with securities regulations in not just one but multiple jurisdictions around the world.

How is this super regulatory feat possible? Because STOs are launched on the blockchain, the typically complex securities issuance process can be rolled into a self-executing smart contract. Tokenizing your assets and selling them off in small chunks to global investors can even be done with a smartphone app.

More practically, you may want to tokenize trading in gold or diamonds so you can track their provenance and movement in the supply chain on the transparent and auditable blockchain. The majority of security tokens issued today are for initial public offerings. Since this new coin on the block is following the rules, the security token offering is already turfing the ICO. By 2019, the days of the unregulated ICO may read like a cautionary tale something like this: During the early blockchain boom, the majority of ICOs were raising billions of dollars and issuing tokens to investors that could be immediately traded or cashed out after the ICO finished. It was pretty obvious that most of those investors, if not all of them, were buying tokens not just because they thought the project was interesting, but because they expected to profit. According to the Securities and Exchange Commission (SEC), that means the tokens are securities.

The SEC usually uses the "Howey Test" to determine whether an investment is a security or not. Here's the official definition:

> ...if you have an investment of money in a common enterprise with a reasonable expectation of profits to be derived from the entrepreneurial or managerial efforts of others, you have a security. Under this test, most token offerings today are offerings of securities. This is particularly true where: (i) tokens are sold to a set of purchasers that is much broader than the set of persons likely to use the tokens in the network; (ii) that purchaser set is passive, that is, it relies on the issuer of the tokens to complete the buildout of the network or to enhance its functionality once it is operational; and (iii) purchasers are seeking returns that don't reasonably correlate with the market value of the goods or services being offered in the network.

Unfortunately, many ICOs meet the Howey Test criteria but did not go through any sort of regulatory approval process before their ICOs, and thus were technically operating illegally. The SEC cracked the hammer down hard, and rightfully so.

The laws we created for securities have been around for decades, but the problem is, they were created during a time before the internet. Blockchain complicates this, which is perhaps why how the regulations affect issuing tokens is not 100% clear, or can be contradictory. For example, ethereum is not considered a security, but many projects are ERC tokens, meaning they're built on top of ethereum.

Owing to these regulatory compliance conundrums, the tale of the ICO could be a short one. Does this mean the end of the Blockchain, too? Absolutely, not! The story of the blockchain digital ledger is destined to endure like the manual double entry ledger system of the Medici dynasty. But future blockchain projects will be financed by the regulatory compliant security token offering.

THREE PLAYERS TO KNOW IN THE TOKENIZED SECURITY SPACE

The good news is that generally speaking governments are being cooperative; they understand that blockchain is a new space and don't want to create complicated rules that could crush innovation, but also want to protect consumers. The solution? The initial coin offering is transforming into the legally compliant security token offering, or STO. Meet some of the players emerging to make it easier for you to issue your token *within* the current legal framework.

1. *Platforms:* These help you launch your STO, raise money and issue your coin, while ensuring you are signing up qualified investors. Examples include Coinlist, Polymath, Harbor and Trusttoken.

2. *Protocols:* Focus on post-issuance governance. They manage who can hold a token, the rejection of transactions and secondary market issuance. Examples include 0x, Swap and Enigma.
3. *Advisory services:* These companies help founders with the top two. Examples include *Harbor* and *CrowdfundX*.

EVOLUTION OR REVOLUTION?

You can argue that tokenized securities are simply an evolution of the current financial system. After all, they are simply digital representations of what we're already doing physically. At least at the start, most of these assets will be tokenized versions of instruments that we're familiar with.

For example, we have "debt tokens" that like a bond or other debt security represent a lending transaction between parties. Instead of signing a piece of paper with the bank or another individual, this would be recorded on the blockchain; the record is immutable. The risk of default could be calculated. That information and data can then be used to create an accurate profile of your financial history. Once all of your assets are on the blockchain as tokens, it's easier for you to put up collateral that has actual liquidity. This is basic, but even at its simplest level it allows for greater efficiency.

SMART STO FUNCTIONS

The embedding of security offerings into smart contracts allows issuers to add many nifty new functions to digital tokens, such as the ability to:

Access global liquidity—STOs can help meet the stricter liquidity requirements of mutual funds as their tokenization, fractionalization and multi-jurisdictional traits make these securities more accessible to a larger global investment base.

Develop programmable equity—Smart contracts can be designed with any function and even to stave off inflation. The PolyMath Token Issuers, for example, can issue different price tranches, and set caps and investment limits, including those for non-accredited investors. A token issuance can be coded to comply with securities regulations or to automatically reject non-qualified investors. The ability to tie new equity (i.e., token) issuance to value creation can help avoid the dot-com high flyers.

Create innovative investor incentive structures—Beyond price appreciation, investors may share in a percent of the revenue and earn rewards.

Launch funds—Fancy operating your own fund? Tokenization platforms will make it possible for anyone to launch not only STOs but also micro funds. On the Enigma Catalyst platform—Blockchain technology developed out of MIT—you can create your own hedge fund. Watch this space closely. Like fractionalization, Enigma's tech demonstrates the vast potential of digital asset creation to democratize investment opportunities.

WILL THE STO BE THE NEW ICO?

Are STOs the future of asset financing? Recent financing activity indicates that, indeed, not only Blockchain startups but also more traditional asset classes are accessing financing through STOs. Real

CHAPTER 6. TOKENIZING THE WORLD

estate is likely to be one of the first big industries that we see unlocked. The Hub—a luxury student residence in South Carolina owned by Convexity Properties—is the first US tokenization of a REIT.[57] The issue was launched on the Harbor token compliance platform, which has recently partnered with the 0x trading platform to create an end-to-end security token issuance platform. The largest benefit to investors is access to liquidity for asset classes that have traditionally been very difficult to buy and sell on a secondary market.

And soon, you may find your STO included in mutual funds, exchange traded funds and other large investment funds—as the more attractive risk-reward proposition of STOs swings the door wide open to the trillion-dollar institutional investor market. The day may be around the corner when 0x and Steem trade alongside Apple and Amazon as top investment fund holdings. Stocks, bonds and other securities may also choose tokenization, or risk being replaced by the more attractive risk profile of STOs in institutional funds. As the ICO deal flow slows, 2019 will be the year of the regulated security token offering.

A NEW BREED OF STABLECOINS IS BUCKING CRYPTO VOLATILITY

Tokenization is opening up closed financial systems to larger liquidity pools. Price risk, though, is still a concern. Beyond the blockchain startups and real estate assets discussed above, anything can be tokenized—films, music, art, commodities and more. By dividing larger assets into smaller fractions, you can invest in any asset that can be tokenized, even those previously off limits to you—like a major

---

57 Jeff John Roberts, "Real Estate on the Blockchain: $20 Million Sale 'Tokenizes' Student Residence," *Fortune*, http://fortune.com/2018/11/27/blockchain-harbor/.

PART III. INVESTING

motion picture. But how do you convince investors to invest money in volatile cryptocurrencies in the film industry?

Even academy award-winning directors need your money. Oliver Stone still struggles to secure financing for some of his films, even though a large adoring public is willing to pay for his opuses. Crowdfunding provides a clever way for these fans to directly fund future filmmakers. Peer-to-peer financing is bringing thousands of films to screens big and small that would never have been made otherwise. Yet still, most film projects don't get made. Less than a quarter of films seeking over $100k succeed and, even then, the average indie film costs $1 million to make.

Since 80 percent of films fail to make a profit, most investors will eschew the additional cryptocurrency risk.[58] The solution is collateralizing crypto. By issuing stablecoins, even Oliver Stone can dust off his political hot potatoes. These digital currencies reduce exposure to cryptocurrency volatility and provide added collateral by backing each token 1:1 by the stable US dollar, or another low volatility asset. The ability to invest in a cryptocurrency collateralized with the price stability of the US dollar is a unique hybrid security previously unavailable to investors.

Digital Collateral

Stablecoins are delivering Satoshi Nakamoto's vision of a peer-to-peer payment system without fraud or double spending. Even the developer of Bitcoin did not foresee the digital coin's disruptive introduction to the world of commerce. The rapid growth in popularity of

---

58 Sergio Sparviero, "Hollywood Creative Accounting:The Success Rate of Major Motion Pictures," *Media Industries Journal*, 2, No. 1 (2015), http://universitaet-salzburg.ac.at/fileadmin/multimedia/Kommunikationswissenschaft/documents/Aktuelles/MedPolitik/mediaindustries_journal2.1.pdf.

cryptocurrencies and a constant flow of new coins have led to erratic adoption rates and trading. Owing to the high volatility, the adoption of the virtual money as a payment method has been slow.

Stablecoins offer a commercially viable medium of exchange by pegging their value to that of an underlying asset such as the US dollar or gold to reduce volatility. Volatility in major currencies is under 1 percent whereas Bitcoin volatility was above 3 percent for most of 2018. These collateralized coins provide the safety of low volatility fiat currencies with the benefits of low cost, transparent and secure digital currency payments.

Three forms of stablecoin collateralization are:

1. Currency—Fiat currency (US dollar-backed Tether (USTD) or Gemini (GUSD)) and cryptocurrencies (Havven (HAV), MakerDAO (DAO)) are the most popular form of collateralization.
2. Algorithmic—Some coins are algorithmically adjusted (Basecoin, Carbon) with changes in supply and demand to maintain a peg, for example, to the US dollar.
3. Digital Assets—A third form of collateralization opening up new forms of financing is digital assets. Many stablecoins use gold for a peg (e.g., Digix (DGX)) but any asset can be tokenized.

Recognizing the ability of stablecoins to reduce a major risk of digital asset financing by lowering cryptocurrency volatility, token issuance platforms backed by stablecoins are being launched. While most stablecoins are used in transactions, TrustToken (TUSD)—a token issuance platform for films, music, real estate and so on—is the next generation of collateralized crypto. The stablecoin has created a bridge between real world assets and crypto investment by providing a platform on which users can tokenize assets and then sell the stable TUSD token to any investor in the world.

To further entice investors, 51% of stablecoins are programmed to provide a dividend or other incentive mechanism.[59] Whether or not the film or other investment is a success, when you want to cash out, you can exchange each token for a US dollar—for parity, more or less.

Because stablecoins lower investment risk, the total crypto market value of the more than 150 stablecoins already in circulation—currently $3 billion, or 1.5% of the total market value of all cryptoassets—is quickly growing (blockchain.com). A new stablecoin is being announced daily, according to the newly formed Stablecoin Association.

How Stable Are Stablecoins?

Investors shouldn't assume an investment in any stablecoin is a safe haven. Although stablecoins have generally done well holding parity with the dollar, they can appreciate or depreciate in value relative to the dollar. If you had invested in the bellwether Stablecoin Tether (USDT), your ride would have been bumpy. Tether's price has been volatile following reports it has not released audits proving reserves equal to the amount of stablecoins issued. Indeed, USDT has stronger price correlation with Bitcoin than stablecoins! Tether, which comprises 93% of stablecoin market value, is slowly ceding market share to new STO entrants providing more collateral and regulatory assurance.

---

59 "The State of Stablecoins," *Blockchain*, https://www.blockchain.com/ru/static/pdf/StablecoinsReportFinal.pdf.

CHAPTER 6. TOKENIZING THE WORLD

Not All Stablecoins Are Alike

The price action in stablecoins differs significantly across coins. Check out the price action during the market downturn in November. As Tether and Bitcoin fell the price of a new breed of coins soared. These newly minted stablecoins have lessened risk by becoming regulated and providing a verifiable audit trail to assure investors the reserves exist to cover withdrawals. Yet each coin has different issuance, collateral and adjustment mechanisms.

TrustToken—the stablecoin platform for tokenizing your assets under your own token—places your asset in a SmartTrust, which serves as a legal entity to comply with financial regulations. To manage your assets, the TrustToken ecosystem provides an open market of trust companies acting as fiduciaries. Since its ICO listing in April, TrustUSD has swiftly climbed into the top 30 ranking on Coinmarketcap. Other newcomers GeminiUSD created by the Winklevoss twins (GUSD) and Paxos (PAX) are registered with the the New York State Department of Financial Services and the New York Banking Law. TrustToken's advantage is the ability to choose a fiduciary in whichever jurisdiction you require from the TrustMarket.

As programmable equity, these coins can be programmed to do some nifty things, like take on hackers. In the case of a security breach, various inbuilt mechanisms have been designed. Gemini has a proxy layer that can halt and reverse coin issuance and transfers in the face of a security incident. When attacked, Dai's (DAI) price sensitivity mechanism triggers a global settlement to minimize losses.

The collateral backing of stablecoins is also being fortified. Dai plans to move from a single to a multi-currency basket of currencies, which will include at least one other stablecoin, the TrustToken. Hybrid models are emerging such as X8Currency backed by 8 fiat currencies

+ gold. carats.io (CARAT) is algorithmically pegged to the Diamond Financial Index (DFI))

The price and volume strength of stablecoins in this most recent bout of high cryptocurrency volatility affirms the role of stablecoins in supporting the wider adoption of cryptocurrencies as a medium of exchange. But it also revealed that not all stablecoins are alike. The price of TUSD, GUSD, PAX, and USDC rose, exhibiting negative price correlation to their forebears Bitcoin and Tether. With this new crop of stablecoins, Satoshi's vision of global e-commerce in which "money can be secure and transactions effortless" has finally arrived.

Chapter 7

THE TRIED AND TRUE PATH TO RICHES: BUILD A CAREER

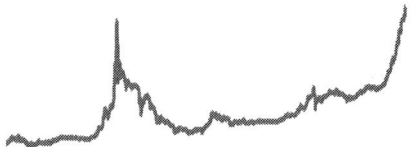

WHY YOU SHOULD GET BLOCKCHAIN CERTIFIED (EVEN IF YOU'RE NOT A DEVELOPER)

The blockchain is one of the highest in-demand, candidate-short industries. But the demand doesn't just apply to developers (who are paid very handsomely). We're seeing demand for industry knowledge across the board: receptionists, shipping clerks, security guards, stock brokers, and marketers.

A mining company is seeking a public relations manager who understands how recording gold sales on the transparent and auditable digital ledger will reduce theft, fraud and murder in conflict mining regions.[60] An investment firm is hiring sales managers who can explain to potential clients how their trading gains will be deposited

---

60 Indeed job posting example 1: https://www.indeed.com/m/viewjob?jk=b01d0c5bbc156ce2&from=serp

PART III. INVESTING

in their digital wallets in real time and available for immediate withdrawal at an ATM.[61]

Bank clerks, travel agents, and shipping clerks will directly transact and track loans, hotel bookings and large cargo shipments with clients and suppliers in secure ecosystems using proprietary tokens to access the secure network. It's happening *now*.

If the blockchain is the fourth industrial revolution—if smart contracts are going to eat the world—job seekers need to be prepared.[62] A worker would not have survived the first industrial revolution without machine tool skills or the information revolution without computer skills. If you master skills for the crypto economy (and are self-aware enough to know in which areas you can contribute), you will have a leg up.

THE BLOCKCHAIN SALARY PREMIUM

Conceivably, your new blockchain career could bring in more revenue than your trading gains. Companies worldwide are paying a premium for in-demand blockchain skills. The shortage of blockchain engineers will soon spread across all disciplines—marketing, finance, logistics, and more. On indeed.com, over 500 blockchain developer positions in the United States, 200 in the United Kingdom, and 90 in Singapore need to be filled. And that's just the tip of the iceberg.

Our organizational structures, functions and even governance structures are changing. Non-tech workers should understand basic

---

61 Indeed job posting example 2: https://www.indeed.com/m/viewjob?jk=ffd007 24162dc775&from=serp
62 Taylor Pearson, "Will Smart Contracts Eat the World?" *Hackernoon*, https://hackernoon.com/will-smart-contracts-eat-the-world-part-one-what-are-smart-contracts-d2cea816035b.

CHAPTER 7. THE TRIED AND TRUE PATH TO RICHES: BUILD A CAREER

blockchain functions such as the role of smart contracts in executing business functions, cryptography in providing security, and mining in transaction processing. If you're a marketer, aim to understand token economics and how incentives and rewards work in DApps.

Austen Allred is the founder of Lambda School, which has trained tens of thousands of programmers. He says that beyond the superficial hype, developers need to understand the tech under the hood. In other words, what are we actually talking about when moving crypto from a to b?[63] The innovative training school is seeing high demand for its graduates who know how to work on smart contracts. Lambda's fee structure enables it to accelerate training in high demand skills. The school provides free training upfront. Students who obtain a job paying $50,000 or more then pay a portion of their salary towards the tuition fee.

Even a basic blockchain certification course can boost your pay. Software engineering salaries are boosted 20 percent for understanding how crypto works, says Allred. Blockchain engineers are the highest paid software engineers, making on average between $150,000 and $175,000 annually, according to Hired. The average software engineer without blockchain training, meanwhile, makes $137k. Those who continue to climb the education ladder to the position of blockchain research scientist are being offered $270,000.

Perhaps the faster road to getting that purple lambo isn't throwing money around with wild speculation, but hard-work, dedication and a good education. There's a thought.

---

63 Austen Allred, "How to Fix Our Broken Education System," *Off the Chain Podcast*, http://offthechain.libsyn.com/austen-allred.

BLOCKCHAIN COURSES FOR THE NON-TECHIE

With a wide choice of blockchain education opportunities, anyone can hone in on the blockchain. Universities around the world have seen a dramatic increase in the number of blockchain and crypto-related courses available.[64] Students around the world will be ready to fill the talent gap. But what about the rest of us?

The good news is that online courses make it easy to become "blockchain certified," while setting flexible study times that fit into your busy schedule. And since Blockchain platforms share in the revenue, you may even make money while training and job searching. Not a bad deal.

B21Block.com is gamifying education on the blockchain and cryptocurrency. When you take one of its six learning blocks, comprising close to 1,000 lectures, you're eligible to receive monthly coin airdrops. You're getting paid to learn.

A good place to start is the B21Block prep course for blockchain certification. By becoming a Certified Bitcoin Professional, you can show potential employers that you have blockchain smarts. Other courses offered cover blockchain and Ethereum developer skills, cryptocurrency investing and trading, and blockchain game development. B21Block.com was founded by bitcoin education pioneer Ravinder Deol, who has become a popular blogger educating "non-technical newbies" on cryptocurrencies.

For those who want to deploy large-scale blockchain solutions within their company, consider getting SAP HANA blockchain development

---

64 "The Rise of Crypto in Higher Education," *The Coinbase Blog*, https://blog.coinbase.com/the-rise-of-crypto-in-higher-education-81b648c2466f.

CHAPTER 7. THE TRIED AND TRUE PATH TO RICHES: BUILD A CAREER

training. Enterprise giant SAP will help you get setup with their blockchain-as-a-service platform.

GET STARTED

To learn more about how you can use blockchain skills and knowledge in your career, join blockchain career groups on LinkedIn. Hub. Careers has a popular blockchain subgroup.[65] Search blockchain job boards such as the CryptoJobsList.

Before you land an interview, attend a blockchain seminar or conference—or two. Read blockchain news to keep up to date. Tell them something they don't know. Send them a list of 10 ideas to improve their business. Once you've got a little bit of experience under your belt, jump in. As one crypto founder said, "The potential that blockchain has on our lives is huge and luckily, it's still day 1."

Aim to find projects that inspire you and work on them as a volunteer—contribute to their GitHub repo, make suggestions, write blogs and be a constant learner. Projects really appreciate community feedback so if you're supportive, proactive and constructive, they will start asking you to play a larger role. And lastly, be ready for a rollercoaster lifestyle.

ADVICE FOR HUNGRY 20-SOMETHINGS WHO WANT TO WORK IN BLOCKCHAIN

The consensus is that learning how to code will give you a big leg up in the space. Basic technical skills go a long way. That said, you don't *have* to come from a technical background. It just helps a lot. But

---

65 Linkedin Hub Careers: https://www.linkedin.com/groups/2881314/profile.

you do have to be passionate, open-minded and willing to reinvent yourself in a new industry. Technology is changing fast. Learn how to learn. Move fast. Oh...and everyone is hiring!

Opportunities are Accessible to Almost All

"...it's still day one. Anyone can start learning now and build a great career out of blockchain quickly." — Sangjin Hong, Cofounder, Chain Cabinet

"The world is your oyster with exciting and lucrative options available that will only multiply going forward. Identify what exactly interests you through self-assessment — Compare options — Consider variables — Prioritize your life — Set Goals — Focus — Go get it!" — Savio Gomez, CEO, Christek IO

But It Ain't Easy

"Developing a career in blockchain isn't easy, especially at the moment due to the bear-market and negative sentiment. However, if you believe this technology is the future, the incentive you have is thinking: what would have happened if I had become an internet expert before the internet exploded?" — Pedro Febrero, Founder @ Bityond (blockchain recruitment)

Step 1: Educate Yourself

"First understand basic economic concepts: what is money? how does it work? what are types of monies? Then read important 20th century economic theory such as the Keynesian's interventionist view vs Hayek's liberal view; organizational theory like how are companies organized, what are communities and crowds or how to create value in communities are concepts important to fully understand as well. Finally learn as much as possible about game-theory, economic incentives, rewards and externalities." — Pedro Febrero Founder @ Bityond

"I would encourage that person to learn as much as they can, attend all the events they can and talk to as many people as possible. Educating yourself is the best thing to do—and find the right area for you to work in Blockchain tech."—Alpesh Doshi, CEO, Fintricity Group

"Look for an institution that offers serious training, try to talk to and keep in touch with professionals who already work in the field and never stop studying and researching, frequent events, build strong and efficient networking with professionals throughout the world."—Paulo Fagundes, CEO @ Datawiz

Step 2: Just Jump In!
"Become a blockchain developer. While it takes time, effort, and aptitude to become a good coder, the industry is moving fast, there is more demand than supply, and there are opportunities for everybody regardless of background or experience, given some maths/science ability and proficiency in one or more of the main world languages including English. Bootstrap your way into a project and learn. And get paid for learning."—CEO and Chief Architect at Pacio Core

"You should find a promising startup, join it and learn—as much as possible. Then, if you're capable enough, you can think about your own startup."—Krzysztof Piech, CEO of a Polish Accelerator

"...One year experience working in the blockchain sector full time is same as four years' experience in more traditional sectors. After two years, you're already considered a senior :) Things are moving very fast. Be smart, adaptive—don't count your hours—and most important, passionate about the technology!"—Mark Couzic, CEO @ Fieldcoin

Chapter 8

WHAT I LEARNED FROM 30 BLOCKCHAIN CEOS

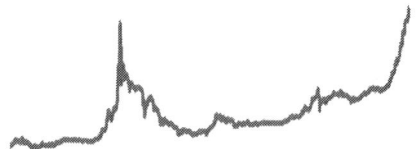

"... I expect universal acceptance of cryptocurrencies worldwide, and their use accordingly. Blockchain technology has already been recognized, now it's turn for cryptocurrencies."
—RASHID YUSSUP, CEO OF TAKLIMAKAN NETWORK

When I reached out to over 30 CEOs running blockchain startups across the world, I wasn't expecting anyone to respond. I wanted to ask them a few simple questions: *What excites them about the industry right now? What advice do they have for a 20-something like me who's just starting out?* I'm fascinated by blockchain and eager to earn more.

To my surprise, nearly everybody got back to me. These blockchain pioneers were—perhaps not surprisingly—open-minded and willing to share their experiences and ideas. Their responses were refreshingly clear, inspiring, and thoughtful, and their insights cut through some of the opium-like exuberance the industry saw in 2018.

For those following the industry, it's valuable industry insight—and perhaps a glimpse of what's to come.

WE'RE LIVING THROUGH A TURNING POINT FOR BLOCKCHAIN

Most of the blockchain leaders who responded were realistic and candid about blockchain's past but remain cautiously optimistic about its present and future. Most of them believe we're living through a pivotal turning point for the industry. We're on the cusp of some really great progress that will redefine how currencies and financial institutions work on a global scale.

"The epic 2017 bull runaway and 2018 crash have gone (we hope!), trust is coming back, and serious blockchain projects are moving forward. We are moving to a new phase of adoption while worldwide experimentation and local regulations are accelerating. Main finance and banking players are entering the market, as well as prestigious institutions (Yale, MIT), and VC funds like Silicon Valley leader Andreessen Horowitz. … We are no longer in the excitement phase but … [we're] getting out of the peak of inflated expectations and entering the disillusionment phase."—Pierre-Alexandre Picard, co-founder at Predicoin

"Blockchain is in the '1,000 flowers blooming phase' of its development. Like the adoption of cloud computing or the early move to the internet, the initial tectonic shifts in the market—and in attitudes—are met with a lot of resistance and some really loud naysayers. The economist Nouriel Roubini recently devoted 37 pages to a rant decrying cryptocurrencies and blockchain as overhyped and criminal. The fact that establishment thinkers are so moved means the cultural shift for a high-trust, low-friction age is coming about." — Dante Disparte, founder of Risk Cooperative

"BLOCKCHAIN IS IN THE '1,000 FLOWERS BLOOMING PHASE' OF ITS DEVELOPMENT."

"Industry leaders, innovators, and regulators must come together to establish a standard that everyone can agree with [and] adhere to. We cannot operate outside our economic and political systems. The blockchain is indeed here to stay. But it won't be able to survive if we (and I mainly mean the tech innovators) refuse to understand or educate themselves about the economy and the policy. They will simply be dead in the water before they get anywhere." — Yassine Anadam, co-founder of Credits

"In Bitcoin we have both SegWit and the Lightning Network's growing adoption, which will decrease transaction fees. In Ethereum we have sharding, plasma, and side-chains that basically enable infinite scalability. From an economics perspective, proper incentives are still lacking, so I would say what excites me the most is the development of better incentives and reward mechanics for crypto-users." — Pedro Febrero, founder of Bityond (blockchain for recruitment)

WHAT'S REALLY BEHIND BLOCKCHAIN'S SUCCESS

It's easy to read a news article and make a quick judgement on the state of blockchain without understanding it. Being a cynic is easy, but most of us don't see what's going on behind the curtain. Tens of thousands of people are pouring blood and sweat into a new industry that will shape the future. One negative news article shouldn't skew your opinion; these pioneers are in it for the long haul.

PART III. INVESTING

Success in the blockchain industry isn't just about financial gains, it's about something much more revelatory and long-lasting.

"I would consider my projects successful if I managed to convince someone out there that it is time to change our monetary system. The tools are finally here for us to change the world and help create a better future for everyone."—Graeme Conradie, CEO of DNX Community

"Success for me is when I look around and see that a positive change has been made in the world due to the efforts of the URAllowance team, our partners, and our community."—Chris Butler, CEO of URallowance

"[Success is about] focus on the long-term impact, instead of near-term price fluctuation and speculation"—Simon Zhu, CEO and co-founder at BitMovio

"Don't rush things. Reputation takes hard work and time to be achieved. Your track record will precede you always. Focus on delivering. … If you do that, success will be the natural consequence."—Paulo Rodrigues, CEO of Stealth Mode Blockchain Startup

"The road to success consists of a combination of joint efforts. The success recipe ingredients are desire, faith, specialized knowledge, imagination, organized planning, and of course, persistence."—Bogdan Maslesa, founder and CEO at UniversalCrypto.org

"The blockchain space is a huge enabler for the financial services industry. It provides the ability to help micro enterprise as well as large multinational businesses. It is nondiscriminatory and helps the wider population participate at the same level as large financial institutions. Naturally, we are most excited about tokenizing securities and bringing a new future and opportunity to businesses both locally and internationally."—Michael Kessler, CEO of Tokenise.io

"At the end of the day, we consider ourselves successful if we managed to make life easier for our users."—Mickaël Fourgeaud, CEO at Primablock

Giuseppe Gori, CEO at Gorbyte, echoed the responses of many others in his summary of what long-term success could look like:

- A worldwide currency that has the stability of a solid fiat currency and no inherent inflation, eventually used as the reference for prices and exchanges. (The ability to maintain fairly stable prices allows the currency to be used for loans, mortgages, salaries, invoices, etc.)
- A currency that is used as electronic cash, not taxed by transaction fees.
- A wallet that is useful to the unbanked of the world, as a savings account accumulating interest and proceeds, allowing them to acquire credit and trade with the rest of the world.
- A wallet that is secure and unhackable, hosted in the user's (dual environment, biometric) device.
- A distributed operating environment that allows easy and secure development of distributed applications without limits on the amount of data exchanged and without the cost of smart contracts.
- The creation of a solid base for the blockchain applications of the future.
- The realization of superconnectivity: a world where things happen for and around people automatically, immediately, and without loading the blockchain with transactions.

BLOCKCHAIN IS STILL A BUSINESS

Building a company is hard. Most startups fail. Hardly anybody I spoke to mentioned financial success as their only goal (although it's important). Instead, they emphasized steady progress over the long term. There are no overnight successes and despite the ridiculous valuations and ICOs we've seen in the past couple of years, the dust is settling and only a few will remain. It's important to keep in mind that while blockchain is disruptive, it's bound by the same rules as most businesses. Blockchain startups need to find good talent, build strong cultures, get their hands dirty in real work, and add actual value.

"Many blockchain professionals in this space lack the business fundamentals, such as valuation models, people management skills, and Agile project management best practices, which then hinders them from being commercially successful."—Daniel Santos, co-founder of DARA

"Everyone expects instant results, especially where new technology is concerned. The reality is that even if the technology is lightning fast and appears to offer new solutions (as blockchain does, for example), we can't forget some of the fundamental basics that have served the business community for centuries. In other words, success does not always come overnight. From our point of view, success comes from building a long-term sustainable business that is not dependent on hype and doesn't feed solely off a speculative bubble. ... It's better to try and work with the financial/business establishment rather than against it. There will be some 'crypto anarchists' out there who will disagree with me, but once you adopt any fixed point of view about anything, you will generally limit your opportunities rather than increase them."—David Honeyman, CEO at Lendo

"DO NOT REINVENT THE WHEEL."

"Remember that blockchain is not the be-all and end-all. It is an enabler, but there are other things out there that need to be considered, and you must look at concepts holistically rather than through blinkered vision."—Michael Kessler, CEO of Tokenise.io

"Make sure that your use case is real before throwing yourself at the opportunity. I think that once the dust settles eventually, we will not talk any longer about 'blockchain development,' but rather just about development. When this happens, you want to be on the sustainable side of this argument."—Mike Scott, CEO and founder of NONA

"As with all the technologies, there are pros and cons. The internet was a boon and bane. So use the internet and blockchain technologies wisely. Look at serviceable products rather than piggy-backing. Do not reinvent the wheel. Look at the landscape of what is being done and the success rate. Use it in conjunction with new technologies like the internet of things and artificial intelligence. That's what will make blockchain potent. As simple as integration of RFID-based tags [radio-frequency identification] to sensor driven devices, blockchain can become the carrier of data bits that is genuine and fast."—Dr. Oji Kikani, founder of Yogin

LOOKING TO THE FUTURE

There's a lot of doom and gloom in this industry: ETH will never scale, the BTC price is too volatile for it to be useful, governments are slowing progress, and so on. Fortunately, a lot of smart people are working to solve these problems. These digital pioneers emanate a lot of excitement and enthusiasm for what's to come.

PART III. INVESTING

"Atomic swaps allow for the exchange of one cryptocurrency for another cryptocurrency without the need for a trusted third party [and will be implemented by BTCP]. After this implementation, it won't be needed for any exchange."—Lucy Louis, strategic partnerships at BTCP

"[For me] non-fungible tokens and tokenization of assets is currently the most exciting. We are at very early stages but every day there are new developments. For example, project ERC1155 is fascinating. Developers involved aim to solve the problem of scalability while merging fungible with non-fungible token functions. A clear advantage of the work done is the exchange of multiple non-fungible [ERC721] tokens in one transaction."—Mark Couzic, CEO at Fieldcoin

"The most exciting thing for us in the blockchain space is the gradual acceptance and adoption of blockchain in the world of financial services. We are actually seeing the U.K. regulatory authority [the FCA] testing various new financial products, such as 'smart bonds' in a welcoming 'sandbox' environment, rather than being hostile toward the new technology."—David Honeyman, CEO at Lendo

"THE OPPORTUNITY FOR IMPACT IS ACCESSIBLE TO ANYONE WHO HAS AMBITION AND CURIOSITY."

"Knowing there are so many talented people in this space makes me super excited about what's going to be released in production over the next five years."—Paulo Rodrigues, CEO of Stealth Mode Blockchain Startup

"I'm excited about infrastructure layer developments, which will improve speed and scalability so that blockchains can cope with large-scale network usage. I'm also really excited to see innovative applications of the technology, which solve real-world issues. Mostly, though, I think it's amazing how many brilliant minds are working in this space, which leaves me inspired every single day."—Jess Houlgrave, co-founder of Codex Protocol

"I am most excited about asset tokenization, especially in the intellectual property space. By tokenizing IP and enabling efficient trading of these tokens, a couple of things can happen: 1) Access is broadened to everyone through fractional ownership and opening up a global market with 24/7 trading, and 2) value is unlocked by unbundling and tokenizing ownership and utility rights separately. For example, in the entertainment space, owners of movie and music intellectual properties do not have any way to easily tokenize these rights. Smart contracts make ownership, usage, and distribution of value programmable through tokenization."—Jeffrey Huang, CEO of Mithril, creator of Machi X, a social crypto exchange that tokenizes IP and enables trading

"We have advanced to the point that the movement cannot be stopped. The fire is lit; it's up to us now to shape that future"—Graeme Conradie, CEO of DNX Community

THREE TIPS FROM DOUGLAS BROUGHTON, CEO OF VENDIBLE

1. If you're in a corporation, build a case for implementing a blockchain solution where you work. Make sure it adds real value, self-form a team at work, and present your case. Be the person who owns the solution.
2. If you want to join a startup and code, make sure you can crush the coding challenge. If you want to join a startup on the marketing, sales, PM side, make sure you have immersed yourself in the culture and can walk-the-walk.

3. But I would encourage anyone who really wants to get into blockchain to first know themselves and what they are passionate about. Chances are there is now a blockchain project centered around that passion. Join the community and start engaging. If your contribution adds value you will quickly find yourself with enough work to fill your day. That's how I started.

REMEMBER TO STAY REAL

"Stay on earth. It's good to have big dreams, it's amazing to want to create something huge..after all that's what a great innovator does. Thinking outside the box. But it will be of no use to you to come up with a solution that is either way too early, or way too old. The secret is in being agile and adaptive and willing to accept change." —Yassine Anadam, Co founder, Credits

PARTING WORDS...
THINK LONG TERM

When we look at inflection points in history, a few stand out—the invention of the wheel, agriculture, the creation of credit and debt (spawning businesses), the industrial revolution, and the internet. Whether or not bitcoin and blockchain fall into this category remains to be seen. However, what we can say is that the floodgates of opportunity have practically opened for everyone. It no longer makes sense to compare cryptocurrencies to Tulip Mania, nor does it make sense to view cryptocurrencies as a fad. We're in new territory and there is still a lot up for grabs, but with an internet connection, research and a little bit of capital, you can participate and profit in the new crypto economy.

The promise of "get-rich-quick" isn't exactly false. Investing in Ether when it was valued at 30 cents would have turned out to be a better investment than investing in Google or Facebook in the seed round—700x within 2-3 years, and fully liquid. And it was open to everybody. Your $1,500 investment in 2015 would have turned into $1,000,000 just two and a half years later. But most people are impatient. When they say "invest in crypto" they expect the price to jump in weeks and have trouble taking temporary losses. The biggest gains are multi-year gains you can earn from letting your coins sit in a hardware wallet and checking back in a few years.

Apart from the specific strategies, if there's one principle you can take away from the book, it's this: *think long-term.* Whether you're trading, investing, creating a business, leveraging a new technology, building a niche—whatever it may be—take a step back and distance yourself from the media hype, naysayers, talking heads, and (sometimes) even your friends and family. Ultimately, you have to make decisions for yourself, and if you can make time to think, take action and cut through the haze with laser-like focus, success is inevitable.

So, how will you choose to use this information? What actions will you take today? You can pick one of the dozens of ideas that I've put forward and find your niche. Perhaps you will try your hand at trading, or apply the lessons learned to become a better trader. Or do your due diligence, make a small investment in a project you deem promising and let it accumulate over a few years. Or your palpable excitement for the industry will move you to dive right in to work for a blockchain startup—plenty are hiring.

Whatever you choose to do, I hope that you use your new-found wealth to do something good, support the community and make the world a better place, whatever that might mean for you as an individual. If you've gotten this far, thanks for reading and I wish you the very best of luck on your journey!

Best,
Misha Yurchenko

AUTHORS LOVE REVIEWS

I do not write for any media outlet or publisher. I publish all my articles and eBooks as an independent author on my blog and across the web. That means I don't have to worry about trying to appeal to a mass audience or selling ads. It gives me the freedom to say what I want and write whatever I think would actually be useful to you, the reader. If you've made it this far and enjoyed the book, I'd greatly appreciate a quick review on Amazon. Thank you!

RESOURCES AND RECOMMENDATIONS

If you prefer to get this list emailed to you, visit the following link: www.mishayurchenko.me/crypto-resources/

Trading
- Coinigy—the best charting tool
- Coinwink—for trade alerts
- Cryptocompare —rankings
- CoinGecko —quantitative rankings
- Exchangify —crypto exchange rankings
- Coinmarketcal—news events, tech releases, ICO's, meet-ups
- Coinrank—analysis of crypto projects through data science
- Protonmail—encrypted email
- WhaleWatch— real time alerts of high volume trades.

Learning
- Jameson Lopp—everything you need to know about bitcoin and more.
- Andreas Antonopoulos is to bitcoin what Michio Kaku is to theoretical physics—a passionate spokesperson and author who has a knack for explaining things. He has some great videos online and a book called Internet of Money.
- Chris Dunn. Free trading/investing videos and content on his site, but the best stuff is a monthly subscription to his daily updates, market reports, live trading rooms, and investment video tutorials.

- Ivan on Tech. Ivan is a blockchain developer with a popular Youtube channel and newsletter. He analyzes individual blockchain projects and measures their current progress, breaks down their fundamentals, and explains concepts in semi-layperson's terms.
- Taklimakan. Access to educational materials, webinars and select products for trading.

Products and Services
- Trezor wallet
- Ledger wallet
- Pepperstone. Crypto asset brokerage services
- Apmex. Buy gold and silver with bitcoin

Who to Follow on Medium
- Hackernoon
- Nathaniel Whittemore
- Chris Burniske
- Michael Casey
- Taylor Pearson
- Coinmonks
- Nassim Taleb
- Daniel Jeffries
- Cotrader

Who to Follow on Twitter
- Vitalik Buterin @VitalikButerin
- Roger Ver @rogerkver
- rock Pierce @brockpierce
- Nick Szabo @NickSzabo4
- Andreas @aantonop
- Charlie Lee @SatoshiLite

- Riccardo Spagni @fluffypony
- Jameson Lopp @lopp
- Gavin Andresen @gavinandresen
- Alvin Lee @onemanatatime
- CryptoHustle @CryptoHustle
- Brian Armstrong @brian_armstrong
- Jihan Wu @JihanWu
- Willy Woo @woonomic
- Pavel Durov @durov
- Tim Draper @TimDraper

Favorite Blockchain (and tech) Podcasts
- Off The Chain (by far my favorite)
- The Flippening
- Tim Ferriss Podcast
- Unchained
- a16z podcast
- Epicenter
- Block Zero
- The Third Web
- The Curious Investor

Videos and Youtube Channels
- The History of Stock Market Crashes
- Principles for Success by Ray Dalio
- How the Economic Machine Works
- Principles of the Yen: Central Bank Documentary
- Bitcoin.com Youtube Channel
- Data Dash
- Tony Vays
- The Modern Investor
- Crypto Daily

- Nomad Capitalist
- Coin Mastery

Best Crypto Newsletters
- The Chain Letter
- Crypto Weekly
- LongRead Sundays
- Token Daily
- Off The Chain
- Unbankd
- Token Economy
- CoinDesk

Investment Platforms Opportunities
- Stansberry Research. Actionable investment recommendations and research for individuals self-managing their portfolios.
- Harbor. STO platform, tokenized real estate.
- Fundrise. Low cost real estate investment platform.
- Polymath. Securities token platform.
- Coinlist. ICO platform and investment platform for accredited investors.

Crypto Exchanges
- Coinbase, @coinbase a US-based exchange
- Bitfinex, @bitfinex a Hong Kong exchange
- Kraken, @krakenfx a US-based exchange
- Bittrex, @BittrexExchange a US-based exchange
- Bithumb, @BithumbOfficial a South Korean exchange
- Idex, @Aurora_dao a decentralized exchange
- Binance, @binance
- Bitmex, @BitMEXdotcom
- Okex, @OKEx
- Bitstamp, @Bitstamp

RESOURCES AND RECOMMENDATIONS

Research and Miscellaneous Tools
- Wallet Explorer. Provides historical, exportable data for Bitcoin wallets.
- Tokendata — ICO performance
- Tokenanalyst.io — on chain transfer value and volume info
- Dappvolume
- MapOfCoins — charting the evolution of cryptoassets
- Bitcoin Volatility Index
- Coinmetrics — useful resources for investors
- Cryptocurrency Alerting — lets you set alerts for ICOs, exchange listings and much more
- Crunchbase for researching deal size, funding, company history and founder profiles.
- AngelList for researching startups and founder profiles

Brain Food: Interesting Articles to Read on a Sunday Afternoon
- The Original Bitcoin Whitepaper
- Ethereum Whitepaper
- Consensusland: A Cryptocurrency Utopia
- Why Bitcoin Matters
- STO Regulations (Reg D, A, CF, etc)
- Bank Failures. Top bank failures.
- Crypto Utopia
- 22 Ideas to Explore with 0x
- Buzz or Innovation? What Explains Bitcoins Returns?
- The Digital Traces of Bubbles
- A Fistful of Bitcoins: Characterizing Payments Among Men with No Names

GLOSSARY OF TERMS

Altcoin: Any cryptocurrency other than Bitcoin or Ethereum.

Capitulation: When investors give up any previous gains by selling their positions during periods of declines. A market correction or bear market often leads investors to capitulate or panic sell.

Dollar-cost Averaging: An investment technique that involves buying a fixed dollar amount of a particular investment on a regular schedule, regardless of the price. As a result you end up purchasing more when prices are low and fewer shares when prices are high. For example, you could commit to add $500 to your retirement fund every month... or buy $300 worth of crypto every month.

Dump/Dumping: Selling away your coins/Downward price movements due to increased selling pressure.

Exchange: Websites where you can buy and sell crypto. Some popular exchanges are Coinbase and Bitrex, Bitflyer in Japan. For a full list of exchanges visit https://list.wiki/Cryptocurrency_Exchanges

FIAT: Government-issued currency, such as the US dollar, Japanese yen or the Euro.

FOMO: Fear of Missing Out. This is a rookie mistake where a coin is skyrocketing and you get the feeling it's gonna pump more, so you buy at the peak (like many did during bitcoin's ascent in 2017).

BULLISH ON BITCOIN

JOMO: Joy Of Missing Out. Opposite of FOMO. You can't make every investment, so once you make a decision to invest, don't regret not making other investments.

Limit Order/Limit Buy/Limit Sell: Orders placed on an exchange to buy or sell a cryptocurrency when the price meets a predetermined amount.

Dead Cat Bounce: A temporary recovery in prices after a huge decrease.

HODL: A misspelling of "hold", means to not sell your cryptocurrencies; alternatively described as meaning Hold On for Dear Life.

ICO: Initial Coin Offering, somewhat similar to an IPO in the non-crypto world. Startups issue their own token in exchange for ether. This is essentially crowdfunding on the ethereum platform.

Market Cap: The total value of a cryptocurrency network, calculated by multiplying the total supply of coins by the current price of an individual unit.

Margin Trading: An act of 'magnifying' the intensity of your trades by risking your existing coins, often equated to gambling, and forbidden on many exchanges.

Mining: The process of trying to 'solve' the next block to obtain an amount of cryptocurrency. In many cases it requires huge amounts of computer processing power

Public Key/Private Key: A cryptographic code that allows a user to receive cryptocurrencies into an account. The public key is made available to everyone via a publicly accessible directory, and the

GLOSSARY OF TERMS

private key remains confidential to its respective owner. Because the key pair is mathematically related, whatever is encrypted with a public key may only be decrypted by its corresponding private key.

Pump & Dump: Price manipulation by whales or collectives. The most famous group is the Palm Beach pump and dump group. Stay clear.

Rekt: A slang version of "wrecked" that refers to losing a lot of your money.

Sidechains: Emerging mechanisms that allow tokens and other digital assets from one blockchain to be securely used in a separate blockchain and then be moved back to the original blockchain if needed.

TA: Technical Analysis, or the analysis of prices based on historical price movements and fancy indicators.

Tokens: Refers to the 'currency' of projects built on the ethereum network that have raised money via issuing their own tokens. Examples:

    0x — ZRX
    REP — Augur
    BAT — Basic Attention Token
    ICN — Iconomi

Shilling/Pumping: Someone essentially advertising another cryptocurrency. If a coin has promised to cure cancer or be the second coming of Jesus, it's being shilled.

Stablecoin: A cryptocurrency with extremely low volatility that can be used to trade against the overall market.

Wallet: Storage of 'keys', or codes, needed to access and use one's coins. There are online ("hot") wallets and offline ("cold") wallets.

Whale: Someone who owns absurd amounts of cryptocurrency.

ACKNOWLEDGEMENTS

Several people made this book possible. Catherine, thank you for working tirelessly to research the strategies and edit the book under insane deadlines—this book truly would have not been much without your help. Rachel, thanks for all your editing, feedback and extremely speedy work. Adina, thanks for taking on this crazy project and working through the holidays to get the book live.

Mark, your insights as a trader pushed me to reframe certain parts of the book and helped step it up a notch. Daniel, your expertise in human behavior taught me a lot about my own psychological fallacies—thanks for pointing them out. And Lorie, nobody would have given this book a second look if it weren't for the cover you made!

I owe a huge thanks (and several bitcoin) to all of you.

P.S. Lastly, why hasn't anyone started a platform similar to Kindle that automatically sends royalties to everyone that contributed to the book? Business opportunity.

Bitcoin Donations
BTC Address: 348H9ntZgXPdS3FFFRAyovvD3vzTFANuLJ

Ethereum/ERC Donations
Eth address: 0xb651287c66fE21eD88cf60fA84f63acae55520fe

LTC Donations
LbaEwuNTkFnsmfL233L2n6Dtxpc7PRLv5F

CONTACT

Questions, comments, suggestions?

Email me at newcryptoeconomy@gmail.com
Join the Facebook Group at
https://www.facebook.com/groups/bullishonbitcoin/

Made in the USA
Middletown, DE
19 February 2019